Affirm press

Sharni Layton's professional netball career spanned fourteen years, including two World Cups with the Australian Diamonds, a Commonwealth Games gold medal and recognition as Australian ANZ Championship Player of the Year in 2016.

In 2018, poor mental health forced Sharni to take a six-month break from sport. In 2019, she switched codes to join the AFLW's Collingwood Magpies, where she made the league's All-Australian team. Sharni now coaches netball and uses her platform to advocate for mental health. *No Apologies* is her first book.

NO APOLOGIES

I dedicate this book to all the strong women in my life, but in particular my Grandma Ellen; Mum, Karin; sister, Kara; and my two beautiful nieces, Aaliyah and Isla. May you follow your heart and dreams, never letting anyone or anything hold you back. You will never fail or fall, because we will always be here to catch you as you learn to spread your wings and bring magic to this world.

Love, Aunty Sharni

Affirmpress
books that leave an impression

Published by Affirm Press in 2021
28 Thistlethwaite Street, South Melbourne,
Boonwurrung Country, VIC 3205.
www.affirmpress.com.au
10 9 8 7 6 5 4 3 2

Title: No Apologies / Sharni Layton and Fiona Harris, authors
ISBN: 9781922400666 (paperback)

 A catalogue record for this
book is available from the
National Library of Australia

Cover design by Luke Causby, Blue Cork
Typeset in Granjon 12.5/17.75 pt by J&M Typesetting
Proudly printed in Australia by Griffin Press

 The paper this book is printed on is certified against the
Forest Stewardship Council® Standards. Griffin Press holds
FSC® chain of custody certification SGS-COC-005088. FSC®
promotes environmentally responsible, socially beneficial
and economically viable management of the world's forests

NO APOLOGIES
SHARNI LAYTON

WITH FIONA HARRIS

STAR NETBALLER
CHAMPION FOOTBALLER
ONLY HUMAN

Affirm
press

Content warning

This book contains strong language and adult themes,
and may not be suitable for children.

It also contains accounts of mental illness, including depression
and anxiety. Some readers may find parts of it triggering
and/or distressing.

If you or anyone you know needs help, contact:
Beyond Blue on 1300 22 4636
Lifeline on 13 11 14
Kids Helpline on 1800 551 800

PREFACE

G'day legends, and thanks for buying my book!

The truth is, I've always wanted to write a book about my life. And if I'm honest, I imagined a three-book series. Yeah, okay, I may have even spent a little bit of time mulling over potential titles for said books. These ended up being my top picks:

Book 1: *Shut up, I'm Sharni!* – because, let's be honest, it's impossible to hear anyone else over the top of me.

Book 2: *Shut up, I'm Captain!* In 2012 I was unexpectedly named Co-Captain of the Adelaide Thunderbirds. While Nat von Bertouch was busy actually leading the team, I was busy crushing the really important duties like flipping the coin at every game. My thumb got a real workout that year.

Book 3: *Shut up, I'm Drunk!* Okay, so I may have been a bit of a wild child when I was younger. I have plenty of embarrassing and stupid stories about the embarrassing and stupid shit I did that prevented me from playing great netball in my youth. Athletes get in a lot of trouble for doing embarrassing and stupid shit when they're drunk, so I've decided to shelve this one until I'm sure it's my last book.

After my agent politely suggested we start with just one book, I knew I needed a title that could cover all of the above ideas, as well as lots of other meaty chunks of goodness and naughtiness. I always seemed to be getting myself into trouble. Not by being mischievous (at least most of the time) but just by being myself. I tried changing who I was at times, but that doesn't work for anyone. So you be you, I will be me, and none of us will apologise for it. 'You do you' is one of my favourite sayings, and I'm a big believer in this philosophy. But, as you'll soon learn, 'me doing me' wasn't always the easiest, or wisest, path.

And for that, I do not apologise!

Enjoy!

Sharni xx

CHAPTER ONE

REBEL YELL

SO MUCH ANGER. My chest is tightening and expanding like a balloon that's about to burst. It's hard to breathe, but no matter how hard I try, I just can't make it deflate.

My eight-year-old brain races at a million miles an hour as I gasp for air. I know that I'm panicking and need to calm down, but there's no space to think rationally. Instead I scream, sob, pull at my hair, punch the ground and finally, exhausted, fall asleep.

'*SHARNI!*'

Mum's voice wakes me. She's somewhere nearby, but it takes a few moments before I work out where I am and what's going on. I'm lying in the back paddock at the end of our road, hidden in the long grass. I start to move, preparing to reveal myself to my worried mother, then I stop. The thought of having another attack is enough to frighten me into staying silent and still for just a little bit longer.

~

That was one of my first panic attacks. They were scary and seemed a bit weird. I mean, I had everything a girl could ask for growing up: a loving family, the beach, sport, pets, friends – I even had a horse, for God's sake. Anyone looking at my happy childhood would probably wonder why this kid started punching the ground and screaming whenever things didn't go her way. Yet, that's exactly what would happen.

Maybe they were childhood tantrums on steroids, or maybe they were an early signifier of things to come in my adulthood. Whatever they were, they were full-on and I felt like I had no control over them. Fury, frustration and panic would surge through me, and I would have no idea why it happened or how to stop it.

There was zero logic to what would trigger an episode like this. It was as if the anger and fear were always there, just beneath the surface, waiting for a random trigger to unleash them. I would just wake up one morning feeling anxious and on edge for no reason, and anything could set me off for the rest of the day.

Mum might ask me to make my bed, and I'd go berserk.

'*I hate you*!' I'd scream. This behaviour never went down well with Mum. And if I was stupid enough to swear at her, she'd hold down my tongue and pour pepper all over it. To this day, I hate pepper.

If I was sent to my room after an angry outburst, which I usually was, I'd kick out the flyscreen on my window and race down to the horse paddock, about 50 metres from our house. There, I'd be free to scream my lungs out and punch a tree without anyone hearing or seeing me except the horses. And boy, I'd punch that tree *hard*. My knuckles would be grazed

4

and bleeding afterwards. But nothing ever hurt as much as the frustration I was feeling inside. The stinging pain in my hand was a welcome distraction from the frightening imbalance I felt in my head and body. It was as if there was a ball of negative energy in me, and I had to let it out.

I always felt better after going three rounds with a tree.

As soon as Mum realised that I'd escaped out the window, she'd march straight down to the paddock to find me and bring me home. By then I'd have calmed down and would act as if nothing had happened.

'Hey, Mum!' I'd say.

She'd give me her tired, patient Mum smile. 'Hey, Sharni. Wanna come back to the house now?'

'Sure!' I'd say, seeming nothing like the kid who'd just screamed the house down and jumped out of her bedroom window.

Mum would put her arm around me, and I'd calmly accompany her back to the house, hungry and ready for dinner. She wouldn't have a bar of being sworn at, but otherwise Mum just seemed to accept these episodes as part and parcel of her Sharni package. This is just one of the reasons I love her so much. It was like she knew I couldn't control my frustration and anger, or even understand them myself. Poor Mum had to deal with 'Sharni's tanties' more than anyone else in my family because Dad and my older sister, Kara, were usually off doing their own thing (basically, anything that didn't involve a kid wreaking havoc).

Funnily enough, I was apparently a pretty chilled-out toddler. The trouble only came when I objected to other people's expectations of how I should behave ... or dress.

It was the morning of the kindergarten photo day. Mum had picked my outfit – a cute black, yellow and white striped dress with a matching yellow bow for my hair – and wanted me to wear it for the photo.

'No way!' I said, folding my arms and backing into a corner.

'Please, Sharni,' Mum pleaded. 'You'll look lovely. Like a little bumblebee.'

'I don't *want* to look like a bumblebee!'

I shouted, pouted and kicked up a full-on stink. I'm sure most mums would be familiar with this scenario. I have no idea how she did it, but Mum eventually convinced her stubborn four-year-old to wear the dress. I trudged off to kinder in a strop, furious with Mum, furious with kinder and furious with the stupid striped bee dress. When Mum got the kinder photos back, she got her first inkling of life with a kid who would not obligingly do something she didn't want to. There, in the back row, and on permanent record for all to see, was a seething bumblebee. The lovely bow was loose and hanging messily across my furrowed brow. In that moment, Mum probably let out a huge sigh – or went and poured herself a strong drink.

By the time I was seven or eight years old, my stubborn streak had evolved into fully-fledged rebellion. There's a good chance I inherited this trait from my dad. Mark 'Big Markos' Layton looked like Merv Hughes and had been a bit of a wild child in his youth. He was expelled from Year Eight for 'getting into a kerfuffle' with his teacher, and once wrote on a footy feedback form that the team he was coaching was 'fucking useless'. Or maybe I got it from my mum, Karin 'Kaz' Layton. She grew up in country Victoria and railed against society's expectations of young women in her area in the sixties. Instead of getting married young and staying at home like other girls her age, Mum went off and got herself a degree in agriculture, then backpacked her way around Europe.

Wherever it came from, I had a clear sense of what I liked – and what I didn't like – from an early age. I loved clothes I could climb, roll and get dirty in. I hated dresses. I loved the outdoors, running, jumping, playing and throwing stuff. I hated sitting inside, and I hated being told what to do.

The Kinder Photo Fiasco was just the start of what was to come.

Times you should apologise #58

When you throw Lego at the fan so you can watch it fly into the wall and take chunks out of the plaster.
(SORRY, MUM)

CHAPTER TWO

YOU CAN'T SIT WITH US

Bonbeach was the best place in the world for a kid to grow up. And no, of *course* I'm not biased. But yeah, it was awesome.

At one end of my street was a pony club, and at the other, a beach. It doesn't get better than that for an outdoorsy kid like me. Bonbeach was a small beach community where we all went to the same school, played in the same netball teams and were all members of the same surf-lifesaving club.

I started in the Little Nippers group when I was four and I loved it. We played games in the sand, paddled and did a lot of wading in and out of the water carrying flags and ropes. You know, all the serious and important four-year-old stuff.

By five years old I was living my best life. Weekdays were spent climbing on equipment at kindergarten and playing in the sandpit, then coming home to Mum's freshly baked muffins. Weekends were spent climbing on anything I could find in my backyard, playing in the dirt and mud at the nearby paddock, and paddling in the water at the lifesaving club. The world was a magical place where every day was one big playtime, and every new kid I met was my new best friend.

Then I started school.

On my first day of prep at Bonbeach Primary in 1993, I approached a group of girls in the yard. 'Hi, I'm Sharni. Can I play with you?'

They stopped playing and looked up at me. And no, they weren't sitting. I was just tall for my age. Like, really tall. At five, I was already around 125 centimetres.

'No,' one of these tiny girls said. 'You're not allowed to play with us.'

I stared, shocked. Up until that point in my short life, I thought kids *had* to play with you when you asked. My lifesaving club friends *always* let me paddle and build sandcastles with them! And even my big sister, Kara, dressed me up like her favourite mini giraffe doll and played games with me after I'd dropped her actual doll in the mud. *'You're not allowed to play with us'* didn't exist in my idyllic life.

Tears pricked at the corners of my eyes, so I quickly turned and ran away. Those short bitches might not think I was good enough to play with them, but there was no way I was going to let them see me cry. Luckily I'd brought John, my teddy bear, to my first day of school, so we went off to play elsewhere.

As I threw John into the top branch of a tree and started climbing up to rescue him, it occurred to me that primary school could potentially suck.

I couldn't understand it at the time, but looking back I can make a few guesses as to why these girls didn't want to play with me:

A. I had a weird, husky 'man' voice.

B. I preferred the shorts and polo shirt of the 'boys' uniform', and refused to wear the school dress.

C. I always had dirt on my knees and had a 'boy' smell.

D. I was freakishly tall for my age and towered over everyone in my class.

I hadn't yet learned how to coordinate my fast-growing limbs, and they caused me – and others – a fair bit of grief on more than one occasion. One day we were all pouring out of the classroom into the schoolyard when a boy tripped over one of my legs and grazed his knee. After that, the kids started calling me 'Spaghetti Legs'. Until that day I'd never been self-conscious about my height, but now I was ashamed of these lanky limbs that I couldn't seem to control.

Over the next few lunchtimes, I spied on different groups of girls from a safe distance. I soon learned that these schoolgirls spent most of their time sitting around making daisy chains or playing mummies and daddies. This wasn't my idea of fun at all. They never ran around, or kicked a ball, or climbed trees, or did any of the stuff I loved to do. *I don't want to play with them anyway,* I thought. *They're boring.*

But I was kidding myself. The rejection hurt. A lot. My self-confidence plummeted, and I spent recess and lunchtimes alone. I was quite shy at that age (hard to believe now!), and kicking a ball along the ground or playing on the equipment by myself felt safer than approaching other kids and being called Spaghetti Legs.

I still had my lifesaving mates on weekends. The Bonbeach Lifesaving Club was my safe place and haven. Unlike school, I could be myself there and it was the one place where I felt like

I belonged. And soon I'd be part of another sports club where I wouldn't feel like a misfit or a loner.

Not long after I started school, Mum – recognising her daughter's need to run, jump and throw things – enrolled me in the local 'NetSetGO' program at the Chelsea Netball Club. Playing netball was what most young girls in my suburb did, so I was familiar with the sport before I stepped foot on a court. Ever since I was a toddler, I'd been sitting on the sidelines watching my mum coach and my sister play every Saturday morning. I'd always itched to join in, and now that I was five, I was officially allowed to play. Unfortunately, I hadn't quite worked out how to make my legs stop moving when I needed them to, which I soon learned was a crucial part of being a good netballer. But I loved jumping and running in a zigzagging fashion all over those old gravel outdoor courts. Although if I took a dive on them, which I often did, I'd end up taking off half the skin on my knees, elbows and chin.

Suddenly I had a new solo activity for those long, lonely lunchtimes. I could practise my goal shooting, just like our coach told us we had to. I was usually put in the defending positions of Goal Defender or Goal Keeper, because of my height, but our coach encouraged us all to practise shooting regardless of our positions.

A few months later, I was wandering across the schoolyard, headed for the goal ring for a solo shooting session, when I walked past a group of boys playing four-square. It looked like fun, but I knew better than to ask if I could join in. So, I sat down a little way away and watched the game. It looked like A LOT of fun. I'd been playing netball for a few weeks by then so assumed I'd kill it – and impress the shit out of the boys – if I joined in. But I was too scared to ask, afraid I'd be rejected again. Instead, I spent every lunchtime over the next couple of days watching them from a distance, inching closer and closer each time.

Just go up and ask to play! the voice in my head shouted at me.

Shut up! I told the voice. *They'll just say no.*

I was paralysed with fear and just couldn't force myself to stand up and go over to them.

One day, in the middle of a game, a couple of the boys suddenly abandoned the four-square game and ran off to play tiggy.

Running! I loved running! Instinctively I jumped up and sprinted after them. They ran straight towards the back fence for a good old-fashioned rock-throwing session and I joined in. Imagine their shock when they looked around to see a tall, gangly girl piffing rocks at the fence alongside them. I saw them looking at me and froze, rock in hand, waiting for them to tell me to piss off. But they didn't. They nodded at me as if to say, 'A girl throwing rocks. Cool.' And that was that. We all went back to pelting the wooden fence with rocks like the five-year-old juvenile delinquents we were. I was overjoyed and relieved. The moment I'd stopped worrying about what *might* happen and acted on my instincts, I'd been accepted. It was another few days before I had the guts to ask if I could play four-square with them.

'Yeah, okay,' they shrugged.

I was so happy I could have burst on the spot. As expected, they were impressed with my four-square skills and agreed to let me play with them every day after that. By Year Three I'd progressed from playing just four-square with the boys to footy and cricket matches on the oval, too. It had taken a bit to convince them that girls *could* play those kinds of 'boy' sports, but when I proved I could match them skill for skill, they accepted me as part of their tribe. Being Queen of Jack in the Pack made me a cool novelty in their eyes. Yes, I may have taken advantage of my height to win a marking contest, but a win was a win! My lanky legs ended up coming in handy after all, and the joy I felt after winning a game definitely outweighed the bad feelings after being teased. All those hours of playing kick-to-kick and driveway cricket with Dad had been worth it.

The girls, however, still wouldn't have a bar of me over those early primary years. They either ignored me, called me names or whispered and giggled whenever I walked past. I tried to ignore them, but it hurt. Being ostracised by the girls was pretty shitty, but thanks to the boys, I slowly started regaining my pre-school grit and self-confidence. In those early years of school, I struggled to understand why I hadn't been born a boy when I was so much more like them than the girls. Everyone knows that the early years of childhood shape our belief systems. We only have our own experiences to learn from, and so we label them as 'true' in our brain because that's our only reality. This is probably why I spent the next few years believing all girls were the devil, even though my sister and the girls at the lifesaving club weren't like that. It was only a handful of girls who were horrible to me, but the experience made me too scared to approach other girls at school after that. It was the boys who had accepted me and, as a result, I had a greater sense of belonging when I was with them.

And I decided that was good enough for me.

Times you *should* apologise #36

When you chase after your sister and whip her with
long sticks all the way home from school.
(SORRY, KARA)

CHAPTER THREE

PLAY LIKE A GIRL

I was eight when my confidence really started peaking. I was feeling more and more comfortable in my tomboy skin, and my love of sport had ramped up even further. I loved any sport. If that sport involved a ball, even better. If I was playing footy, cricket, netball or paddling out on my board in the waves, I was happy and in my element. There was no better feeling than moving my body and making it do what I wanted it to. And winning.

Man, I loved winning.

My extensive list of sporting activities in upper primary school included:

- netball
- cricket
- swimming
- wrestling (this was just me and my male cousins on a Sunday arvo)
- surf lifesaving
- basketball (only one season … I hated it)

- skateboarding
- horseriding.

Every single race, game and warm-up was a competition for me. I'd be tempted to say that it was obvious I was destined to be a professional athlete, except for the fact that professional female athletes didn't really exist in most sports back then. If I *had* entertained the idea of a sports career at that age, it would probably have been as a ball girl in tennis games. These were the only females I was exposed to who were associated with professional sport at a young age. I had no female athletes to look up to or to model myself on, so I was playing purely for the love of these sports and the competition.

'First one to the boathouse and back wins!' my lifesaving coach would yell, and I'd be off and running. There didn't need to be any kind of incentive either. Awards and medals were cool, but I just wanted to win, or at the very least be a front-runner.

I've never been a fan of 'participation awards', or of the idea of getting rid of the scoring system in junior sport. Competitive sport teaches kids so many great life lessons, and hey, life's not fair. It just isn't. You have to fight to win. I'm lucky that I learned this lesson at a young age.

There was no better feeling than using the muscles in my body and feeling fit and strong. Having a body that did what I asked of it gave me a feeling of invincibility, and that it was doing what it was created to do. The more I ran and played, the more energy I had. It gave me a sense of freedom, like it was the closest I could get to flying.

Summers were spent at the Bonbeach Lifesaving Club.

Even if my mates and I weren't competing or training, we'd go down there just to hang out. Surfing carnivals, Nippers training, open-water swim events, sausage sizzles, trivia nights – there was always something going on. I'd write BONBEACH down my leg in permanent marker during carnivals and try to keep it on as long as possible after the event. I was super proud of my club. During events we'd all be racing around the water buoy killing ourselves laughing as we pushed each other off the boards and tugged at each other's feet.

I've always had an awkward running style. My knees go in and my legs swing out (for anyone who has seen me run or play, you know what I'm talking about!) and I look a bit weird.

Despite winning the beach sprints and flags at lifesaving, I always felt self-conscious about the way I ran, especially when I noticed that the other kids' footprints in the sand were all straight, while mine faced out like duck feet. I'd try my hardest to force my feet to point straight, but I just couldn't do it. My spaghetti legs, combined with my duck running, made it hard to be speedy in a long-distance race, but I'd push my gangly body as hard and fast as it could go. I always kicked arse when it came to sprints. Those long duck-footed strides gave me a great advantage.

I was lucky to have been gifted with athletic ability as a kid, but my mindset was a huge part of it as well. Losing just wasn't an option for me. I always went into both individual and team events believing that I was, or that we were, awesome. When I was moving my body and exercising, competitive or not, my mind was calm and still. The meanies, the anger, the problems and the stress all went away. It was just the sand beneath my feet and the taste of salt in my mouth, from sweat or seawater. That was all that mattered.

On the netball court, I loved the feeling of jumping in the air for a rebound goal or intercepting a ball as it whizzed through the air towards my opponent. The Chelsea Netball Club was a small association where everyone knew everyone, and my team – the Bonbeach Stingrays – was made up of kids from my lifesaving club and school. And by the time I was in Year Four, it was obvious to everyone that I wasn't too shabby at this netball thing. I accumulated so many Best and Fairest trophies that I ran out of room on my bedroom shelves. Netball was fun and I loved it. I spent every Saturday playing, rain, hail or shine. The atmosphere was always electric, too. Parents would be screaming, whistles would be blowing, and the smell of sizzling sausages was in the air. And the best part? Mum always bought me a hot dog and Coke after a game.

I desperately wanted to play Auskick football, but I was already playing every sport under the sun by the time I was eleven, so Mum said I couldn't fit it in. Instead, I had to settle for regular games of backyard footy with my cousin and his mates. They never took it easy on me because I was a girl, which I appreciated. They'd tackle me to the ground, whack me in the head with the ball and hold me face-down in the dirt, and I felt honoured. Then I'd push them off and punch them in the guts.

I was good at football. Really good. I could tackle, break a tackle, had a bombing kick and could mark a ball over the top of anyone.

I'm pretty sure I could be the next Gary Ablett, I'd think to myself. *I can take speckies, kick goals and be an all-round AFL hero, too.*

I was one of the best footballers at school and was also the opening bowler for my cricket team in Parkdale (the only girl in my league) and played with Scott Bowland who went on to play T20 and state cricket. It never occurred to me that I wouldn't be able to play with the professionals as a girl. After all, I was already doing it.

As a sporty kid, the idea of playing a major sport on a big stage with loads of people watching seemed pretty cool to me. When the 1996 Atlanta Olympics came along, my friends and I talked non-stop about the events and obsessed over which Aussie athletes we liked best, including Cathy Freeman, Susie O'Neill, Nicole Livingstone and Gillian Rolton. These women were our superheroes. They were chicks *and* they were playing sport on TV. Amazing. I watched Gillian Rolton fall off her horse during cross-country, get back on, fall off again, get back on and finish the course with a broken collarbone and multiple broken ribs so that Australia could win the gold medal.

Now *that* was a superhero!

As I sat cross-legged on the lounge-room floor watching the Olympics, I had an epiphany. You didn't have to be a man to be successful in sports. You could be a champion sportsWOMAN. And that's what I wanted to be.

The question was, how did I, Sharni Layton, get to that level? How could I get to the Olympics and join these incredible athletes?

But hang on, where did they all go? I'd spent two weeks watching all these amazing women compete for what felt like twenty-four hours a day, seven days a week, then they had the closing ceremony and that was it. My golden girls were gone, and I had to say goodbye to the heroines I'd fallen in love with. Some I wouldn't see for another four years; others would retire, and I'd never see them again.

I fell back into watching AFL and cricket and forgot for a little while that it was possible to be a woman on the sporting world stage. I rekindled my dreams of being Jason Dunstall, a big, balding goal-kicking machine, and of playing cricket for Australia one day.

Then I turned twelve.

'Sorry Sharni, you're not allowed to play cricket anymore.'

I'd hit the age when playing with boys was no longer an option. Was I shitty about this? Yeah, a little bit. But I was also too young to see the inequality and prejudice behind the reasons why I could no longer play. I was still playing netball, basketball, and competing in horseriding (more on that later) and surf lifesaving, so something had to give eventually. But being forced out of cricket left a bad taste in my mouth. I missed it and I started getting frustrated when watching footy and cricket on the telly, the only sports I remember seeing on TV in the nineties. Netball was televised on the ABC back then, but that was a 'boring adult news channel' so I avoided it when channel-surfing. (I'm now an ABCTV-aholic).

I was twelve and watching a sport on TV that had been taken away from me (cricket), and another sport that girls didn't play at all (footy). Where were all the women? Where were *my* role models?

Then the year 2000 came along and changed everything. It was my final year of primary school and there was an excited buzz in the salty Bonbeach air. The Olympics were coming – to Sydney this time – and I was so excited to see my hero female athletes again. There was so much hype around the opening ceremony and we, along with the rest of the world, couldn't wait to watch it.

I couldn't believe the Olympics were in our own backyard! Mum, Dad, Kara and I cuddled up on the couch to watch Nikki Webster fly into the stadium blowing strawberry kisses, and Andrew Gaze walk out waving his big Australian flag, rocking his role as Australia's favourite male athlete and dad. Just when I thought the night couldn't get any better, Cathy Freeman appeared in all her amazing glory. Our very own Australian spiritual goddess. Cathy was our idol, our icon, our everything for these Olympics. I watched in awe as she lit the ring of fire and water poured down all around her. Time stopped for this twelve-year-old, sitting on her couch, eyes wide. I knew then that these Olympics would be a game changer for the world, and for me.

In that moment, my focus shifted. Screw the men. I wanted to be like Cathy. But how did I do that? There was no netball in the Olympics, and my swimming was good, but there was no way it was 'Olympics' good. I did love horses, and I was an excellent rider. So, equestrian it was! Suddenly I knew what I was going to do when I grew up. I'd ride in the Olympics, become a vet and have a huge farm with stables and ponies. That was the dream (in that order). My new goal was set in stone. I was 100 per cent certain that I'd represent Australia and win gold for my country one day. I had no idea how I was going to make that a reality, but that didn't matter.

I'd figure out those details later, no biggie.

Times you should apologise # 77

When I was grumpy for my teacher because I snuck from my room to the lounge (after Mum and Dad went to bed) to watch the Olympics until 3am.
(SORRY, MS ROSE)

CHAPTER FOUR

MY FIRST LOVE

Mum grew up riding horses in Mansfield and started volunteering for the Riding for the Disabled program in Clayton when I was a toddler. The first time I laid eyes on a horse, it was love. When Mum propped me up on top of one of these magnificent beasts, I knew horses had officially captured my heart. Unfortunately, there was no way the Layton family could afford a horse of its own, so I had to be content tagging along with Mum to get my horse fix. Lucky for me there were a lot of paddocks around Bonbeach where a few friends kept horses. I loved going down to pat our horsey neighbours and feed them apples over the fence.

One family friend, Emily, owned a beautiful horse named Sandy, and I'd been insanely jealous of her for as long as I could remember. One day we were in the car when Mum turned to me and said, 'Emily has grown out of her horse and she's up for free lease.'

My eight-year-old heart almost leapt out of my chest. Did this mean what I thought it did?

'Do you want to give horseriding a go?'

'ARE YOU KIDDING?! MY VERY OWN HORSE?!'

I was so excited I may have done a tiny bit of wee in my pants.

Taking over the lease of a horse was the best possible scenario for a family like ours who didn't have bucketloads of cash lying around. I could feed, ride and take care of Sandy, but we didn't have to pay a cent because technically we didn't own her. Horses are bloody expensive so everyone, especially Mum and Dad, was very happy with this arrangement.

I immediately joined the pony club at the end of my street, and any free time I had was spent there or at the paddock 50 metres from our house where I kept Sandy. Behind the pony club was a bike track that ran through the wetlands all the way to Mordialloc, which in the nineties was all farmland. My pony club mates and I would ride our horses through the back paddocks to the Edithvale McDonald's and, once there, we'd walk our horses straight into the drive-through lane and up to the speaker.

'One Happy Meal, thanks!'

We loved watching the employees' startled expressions as we trotted up to the window one by one to collect our orders. It was especially entertaining when our horses stuck their heads through to say hello to everyone inside.

One day, Sandy took a huge dump right in the middle of the drive-through lane, in front of five waiting cars. Within seconds, the furious manager appeared, plastic bag in hand.

'PICK IT UP!' he roared.

My friends almost wet themselves laughing as I dismounted, red-faced. I started scooping the steaming hot poo into the thin plastic bag, as impatient drivers honked at me to hurry up and get out of the way. I didn't have much of an appetite for my Quarter Pounder after that.

On another Maccas outing, I went to hop back on another horse I had, Goldie, after we'd finished our lunch, but she wouldn't let me. The closer I got to her, the nuttier she went. Suddenly, she reared up on her hindquarters and, with me still holding the reins, spun me around like I was on a psychotic merry-go-round. I lost my grip, hit the ground and looked up just in time to see Goldie bolting away. I jumped up to chase her, but Goldie was off and running. I raced to the road, hailed down a passing car and jumped in.

'Follow that horse!' I shouted.

I assumed Goldie was heading back to the pony club, and the thought of her galloping across two main roads in front of oncoming traffic horrified me. I sat in this stranger's car, my stress levels off the charts, directing them towards the pony club, my Macca's cup still in my hand.

When we got to the club, I was relieved to see Goldie safe and well, happily cantering around with another girl on her back. The people there had been more than a little surprised to see a solo Goldie casually trotting into the stables, but were more worried about where I was! That whole back area of Edithvale is now built up with houses and apartments, so I'm grateful to have had those special times with my horses and mates. A couple of years after leasing Sandy and Goldie, I took over the lease of another horse, Billy. Sadly, I'd grown too tall for Sandy and Goldie was clearly a bit nutty, so I needed to find a horse that would fit my long body.

Having horses as a kid is awesome for many reasons. They teach you responsibility, for one. If the weather was hot, I had to make sure I took their rugs off in the morning, then remember to put them back on at night. I had to feed, ride and groom them daily, too. Although, I wasn't *always* as responsible as I should have been.

By Year Four I'd made friends with a few girls at school. Rebecca and Peta-Mae were in the year above me and they also loved kicking balls, running around and throwing stuff, so we became good mates. Peta was a good rider, too, so we'd double-dink and do jumps with both of us on Billy's back. Not the smartest idea, but we found it hilarious at the time, especially when one of us fell off. So, yeah, not *always* responsible.

Another time, I told Rebecca the fence wasn't electric (knowing full well that it was) then fell on the ground laughing as she touched it and was immediately catapulted three feet into the air.

'Oh my God,' she said, lying on the ground looking dazed and confused. 'Did you just whack me in the back with a cricket bat?'

Not a prank I'd recommend to kids now, but I found it hilarious at the time.

On the days when I was competing in horse events, Mum would wake me at 4.30am and I'd walk to the car, zombie-like, and sleep the whole way while Mum drove. Two-day events at Werribee and Wandin were the most fun. Everyone from the pony club would camp together and there was always a dance party on the Saturday night. Us kids would rock the night away, and the parents had their own fun back at the campsite. Observing a bunch of hungover adults trying to stay awake and not throw up during the event the next day was always a highlight.

As most 'horsey people' know, the bond you have with a horse is like no other. There's no better feeling than riding your horse towards a five-foot-high fence and instinctively knowing it's going to jump over it because they trust you. Unless he gets stage fright on the one occasion in four years when your dad decides to come and watch your event.

Dad was always supportive of my sporting activities when I was a kid but wasn't around for most of my games and competitions because of his busy work schedule. He thought I was only doing horseriding because Mum forced me into it, so he rarely came to my events. I was twelve before Dad finally attended one. And this happened to be the day I was riding Goldie. Sometimes she'd do exactly what I wanted her to, but other times … not so much. That day, with Dad watching, Goldie stopped at a jump three times during the showjumping ring event. In line with the rules, I was eliminated on the spot and told to leave the ring. As I trotted out past Dad, he made a smart-arse remark and that familiar surge of rage rose inside me.

'*Go and get fucked!*' I snapped.

The words flew out of my mouth before I could stop them. I'd sworn at Mum, but she wasn't scary like Dad. I had *never* spoken back to my father, let alone sworn at him. Dad and I were as shocked as each other. My first reaction was panic, so I kicked my horse into a canter, bolted to the other end of the horse paddock and stayed up there until I knew Dad had left. The incident was never mentioned again, and it was only years later that I learned Dad had actually cracked up as I bolted away and decided his daughter's fear of the repercussions was punishment enough.

Mum and Dad both worked during the week, so my sister and I would always walk home from school together. As soon as we were in the door, I'd ditch my bag and head straight down to the horse paddock. I'd either bring Sandy and Billy to the house to saddle them up (sometimes I'd even put my dog up on one of the horses for fun) or carry a saddle down the road and call for one of them from the top end of the paddock.

'BIIIILLLLLLLYYYYYYYYY!'

They'd always hear me … as would anyone else within five suburbs.

One of the residents from the caravan park next to the paddock was chatting to my mum one day over the fence. 'I often hear a man calling out to his horse, Billy, in the paddock,' he said.

'That "man" is my twelve-year-old daughter,' Mum told him.

Times you should apologise #87

When you think it's funny to put your tiny fox terrier up on your horse's back when she's too small to jump down.
(SORRY, NICKY)

CHAPTER FIVE

BUT I DON'T WANNA BE A COWGIRL

To the delight of everyone in my family, puberty hit and my stubborn and strong-willed nature began to ramp up. This also came with a healthy side of angry episodes and panic attacks. Good times in the Layton household.

Around the same period as the infamous 'Go and get fucked, Dad' incident, I was at a pony club rally when my horse refused to do what I wanted it to. For the first time, I lost my shit in public. As I felt my chest tightening and the rage inside me growing, I jumped off Billy, took off my helmet and threw it to the ground as hard as I could.

'WHY WON'T YOU JUST DO WHAT I WANT, YOU STUPID HORSE?!' I yelled. *'HOW FUCKING HARD IS IT TO JUST DO WHAT YOU'RE TOLD?!'*

Mum was undoubtedly thinking the same thing about me at that moment.

Dozens of shocked faces stared at me as I stomped away, leaving my horse standing alone. Thankfully Billy was an amazing horse and was completely unfazed by his idiot tween rider. Everyone else was probably thinking, 'Um … what do we do with this horse now?'

As always, Mumma Kaz was there to pick up the pieces, walking Billy back to the stables while I saw my tantrum out.

The Billy meltdown was the beginning of me having the occasional tanty in public, instead of just at home. When I felt the crazy emotions building up, I just started to let them out, no matter who was around. Mum knew how to deal with me by this time, but still put up a fight now and again.

When I was cast as a cowgirl in the Year Five school play, we faced off in a mother–daughter showdown when I insisted on dressing as a cowboy.

'You were cast as a cowgirl, not a cowboy,' Mum told me.

'But I don't *want* to be a cowgirl!' I shouted.

I won that fight, making my stage debut as a very manly, very happy, cowboy. I even drew on a thick black moustache, just like my dad's.

My sister Kara and I had always been complete opposites, but now that she was in high school and I was the annoying kid sister, our fights became more intense. I'd spent years watching my super-popular, super-cool blonde teenage sister with a mixture of awe and jealousy. My sister always looked amazing and had no problem making friends or getting boyfriends. These were only some of the reasons why I made her life a living hell by regularly punching her or stealing her new clothes and bringing them back caked in mud.

But Kara and I always had each other's backs when it really mattered. Home alone one day, we got into a fight and I punched her as hard as I could then ran away. Not hearing her behind me, I turned to walk back down the hallway when Kara suddenly leapt out of her room brandishing a hairbrush. She piffed it straight at my head, and it cut my cheek open. As blood started gushing out of my face, we stared at each other in horrified silence. Mum was gonna be SO pissed!

'What happened to your face?!' Mum cried when she got home a couple of hours later.

'I fell over,' I said.

We had no problem beating the shit out of each other when our parents weren't around, but we'd never tell on each other. That would be rude.

By my last year of primary school, I'd somehow made the transition from 'loser girl' to 'cool girl' in the eyes of the Year Six female cohort. I soon worked out that this had little to do with me, and more to do with these girls being suddenly very interested in the Year Six male cohort. And who was hanging out with that lot? This gal!

It was also the year when I had my first 'boyfriend', because that's what we did in Year Six. Of course, none of us had any clue what being a boyfriend or girlfriend actually meant. All I knew was that kissing was disgusting. Like, just horrific. What twelve-year-old girl wanted a boy to shove his tongue in her mouth? I couldn't believe adults did this stuff all the time *for fun*! I vowed never to let a boy catch me in a game of 'kiss chasey' ever again.

Of my many 'I refuse to be a girl' childhood moments, my favourite is Year Six graduation. When I, once again, refused to wear a dress, Mum had flashbacks to that long-ago and traumatic Kinder Photo Fiasco. But this time she really put her foot down and said that if I didn't wear a dress, I couldn't go. We finally came to a compromise when I found a dress with a hood attached. Happy days.

At this age, I wanted to wear jodhpurs twenty-four seven, pierce my nose and cut my hair so it was short and spiky, because that's how all the cool boys wore it. Unfortunately, Mum wouldn't let me do any of these things. She was still trying to nudge me towards being a girly girl, and do girly-girl things, at least some of the time.

Strangely enough, just at the time when I was wishing I was a boy, my voice matured even further into its deep, manly tone. Many times, I'd answer the home phone with a cheery, 'Hi, you've called the Layton household.'

'Mark, it's Bob!' I'd hear someone say. 'How's it going?'

'Hey, Bob, this is Mark's daughter Sharni,' I said, 'but I'll go get Dad for you.'

My cute, husky little-kid voice developed into a deep baritone by the time I hit puberty and being mistaken for a man over the phone soon became a common occurrence.

I might not have been as comfortable with my voice if I hadn't grown up listening to the female Aussie radio broadcaster Tracy Bartram. I loved Tracy. Her voice was deep and loud just like mine, and she was on the radio, which meant it must be cool for girls to have a deep and husky voice.

But I had bigger things to worry about than my deep voice and arguments about wearing dresses. Because I was about to start high school.

Times you should apologise #39

When your Year Six boyfriend gives you flowers for Valentine's Day and you're so embarrassed that you shove them in your bag so no-one can see them.

(SORRY, JAMIE)

CHAPTER SIX

TEEN ANGST

When Mum told me she had enrolled me in Mentone Girls' Secondary College, I was pissed. My school friends were going off to Patterson River Secondary College, and most of my lifesaving mates were heading to Mordialloc Secondary College. NO-ONE was going to Mentone Girls'. I had no idea that Mum had worked her arse off to get me into a good school that was out of our zone, so in one of my usual 'Sharni tanties' I begged her not to send me. Mum struck a deal with me. If I hated Mentone after a year, she'd let me go to Patterson River at the start of Year Eight. It wasn't my ideal scenario, but it was the best I was going to get, so I shut up and agreed to go … for ONE YEAR!

(I ended up staying the entire six years. Mum was right. Again.)

Mentone Girls' Secondary was huge, and there were more kids in Year Seven than there had been at my entire primary school. I looked around the colossal hall on that first morning and, for the first time in my life, felt very small. After a few minutes, a short girl with short hair to match and a friendly grin walked up to me.

'Hi, I'm Katie!'

'I'm Sharni.'

'Do you know anyone?'

'No. You?'

'Nup. Wanna hang out?'

'Sure.'

We smiled at each other and were inseparable for the next six years.

Katie and I had a lot in common. We both wore boys' jeans or jodhpurs, Blink-182 hoodies, belts with pocket chains, and spiky bracelets. I didn't know any other girls like me who skated and listened to rock bands like Linkin Park, Papa Roach and Limp Bizkit. But when I met Katie, she soon introduced me to similar bands like Blink-182 and Bodyjar, and I realised then that we were destined to be friends for life.

I was lucky to have a best friend like Katie in those first few years of high school, especially when no-one we hung out with at Mentone Girls' lived in my area. This made it hard to maintain friendships outside of school hours. I spent holidays with my old crew from Bonbeach, but they all went to Mordy High together, so there were a lot of inside jokes and banter I could never be a part of. As a result, I felt stuck between two camps – the school group and the Bonbeach group – and didn't feel like I fitted 100 per cent in either one. But I always had Katie as my constant companion in those early high school years, so I was happy.

Under-age dance parties were all the rage in my area growing up, but we preferred concerts. Blink-182 came to Melbourne when we were in Year Seven, and Katie and I were desperate to go. After a few phone calls back and forth between our mums, we were ecstatic when they said they'd bought us tickets and that they'd drop us off and pick us up. Kara was furious. At fifteen, Mum had only just started letting her go to the under-age dance parties in Frankston, and here I was going to a concert in the city at twelve. I, of course, claim to this day that Mum made this decision because I was the more responsible child.

That Blink-182 concert was the start of Katie's lifelong love of live music. She became completely obsessed with the whole scene and, as her best friend, I reaped the rewards of her hard-rock habit. Whenever there was a live music event happening near us, Katie and I were there. From Battle of the Bands to Sum 41 at the Corner Hotel, we saw them all. Katie was the queen of winning concert-ticket giveaways on the radio, and one time she scored us tickets to Triple M Radio's M One Concert, a gig we remember fondly to this day.

I was six feet tall and Katie was five-foot-nothing, a fact that I endlessly used to my wicked advantage. I tormented my poor friend endlessly, hiding her pencil case, books and folders in places she would never be able to reach. Once I shoved a bunch of her favourite pens through some holes in the classroom ceiling and left them there all day. In the end, our teacher made me get the pens out because she couldn't reach them either.

Mentone Girls' Secondary was a twenty-minute train ride from my house and another twenty-minute walk from the station, so every morning, Kara and I would get the train in together and make a few pit stops on our walk to school. First, we'd duck into Woolies and fill up a lolly bag, devouring the entire contents as we wandered the aisles. Next, we popped into Bakers Delight to spend our weekly train money on a sixpack of doughnuts.

The owner loved us and always sold us cheesymite scrolls for the bargain price of one dollar. My active lifestyle was the only thing that saved me from ending up like Bruce Bogtrotter from *Matilda* by the time I finished Year Seven.

I had entered high school as a smart kid who always behaved well in class and did her work. Halfway through Year Seven I decided that was lame. I was going to try and fit in with the cool kids instead. Overnight I became a loudmouth smart-arse, talking back to the teachers to make my classmates laugh (and therefore like me). Detentions began flying my way and continued to do so over the next few years. Now I can see what a dick I was and deeply regret my idiotic behaviour. Schoolwork had always come so naturally to me, but when I stopped paying attention it was hard to catch up, especially as I got into the later years of high school.

I also had less time to study because my sporting schedule became even more full-on once I started high school. I was still looking after my horses and entering events, but I had also started trialling for, and making, the Chelsea Netball Club squad teams in the Under 15 age group.

I was still the tallest girl on my netball team and playing in defender positions. On squad tournament weekends we'd play six or seven games a day. My fondest memories of those times were the treats Mum would buy us: Bakers Delight scones and cheesymite scrolls, Tim Tams and Starburst lollies. We'd be obsessing about the sweet treats while we were on the court, and the promise of all that sugary goodness would spur us on! My main source of motivation was food, and it still is to this day. I love food. As a teenager, I never had an issue with putting on weight because I did so much sport and had a ridiculously good metabolism. Like most teenage girls, I was self-conscious about my size, but my insecurities were around my height, not my weight, and I had a healthy relationship with food. It wouldn't be until much later that my relationship with food would become an issue.

The netball club was a fun place to congregate at nine o'clock on a Saturday morning, and we'd stay there until mid-afternoon, playing games and then umpiring. I made $10 per game when I umpired, enough to buy a coke and a hot dog with my *own money* (so exciting!). If we had a game off, we'd run over to the park beside the courts to play there until it was time to go back.

I spent many nights trialling for State League teams and wondering if I'd make the cut, but more often than not I didn't. I was good, but not good enough, and many times I missed out on making the State League A teams. I wanted to be in the A team, of course, but I just wasn't an A-team kind of girl, apparently, and that was fine with me. Anyway, I loved being part of the B team. The girls were great, and we had a lot of fun when we were playing games, win, lose or draw. Most times we ended up winning – obviously the preferred outcome – but even when we lost it wasn't as big a deal in the B grade. It was disappointing to be constantly overlooked by the A-grade people, but it also meant I didn't take the sport too seriously. I was still an excellent netballer compared to a lot of girls my age and I was happy enough with that.

Boys were the last thing on my mind in those first few years of high school. Sure, some may say this was because I was never asked out by any, but whatever. Shut up.

The truth is that it's tough to meet boys when you go to an all-girls school. Out of the five schools in our area, ours was known as the 'Mattress School' (the slums), which made it even harder. The only place girls from Mentone Secondary could hope to meet boys was at the local train station.

Mentone train station was a total meat market for all five high schools in the area. As soon as the final bell went, make-up would magically appear on girls' faces, and skirts would become two inches higher as we all made our way there. Teenage dramas played out on the ramps, against the wire fences and at the far ends of the platforms every weekday.

'She likes him,' ... *'He thinks she's cute,'* ... *'They're making out in the underpass.'*

It was all way too intimidating for a sporty tomboy from Bonbeach. All I knew about boys was how to take the piss with them and rub their faces in the dirt. I had no clue how to flirt with them. My school dress did end up shorter than it should have been, but this wasn't because I was ever a girl to hitch up her skirt. It was because my legs just kept growing and growing, and I wondered if they'd ever stop.

I was so tall that I didn't fit into girls' jeans anymore. The ones I tried on weren't just ankle freezers, they were calf freezers. And unfortunately, seven-eighths tights weren't yet a thing in the early noughties. The only jeans I found that fitted me were boys' jeans, so baggy jeans became my go-to. Even though I preferred wearing boys' clothes, the lack of options definitely contributed to my crappy self-confidence in Year Seven. At twelve years old, I was six feet tall with a size-eleven foot. Girls' clothes didn't fit me, so I couldn't wear them even if I wanted to.

Mum drove me up to the city one day in the hope that we'd find some 'nice' clothes. After hours of trying on jeans and tops, none of which fitted me, I eventually broke. In that moment it felt as if I was destined to never fit in, literally or figuratively, with my peers. Soon after this, Mum found a shop on Chapel Street that specialised in 'tall girl' clothes and shoes. This store ended up being the only place I found girls' clothes and shoes that fitted me. By that time, though, I'd made up my mind that there was no point trying to find 'nice' girls' clothes when I was tall, lanky and awkward anyway.

Stuff it! I thought. *I'll just wear boys' jeans.*

Mum understood that I was struggling with all of these insecurities and, in an effort to flip my thinking and help me see my height as a positive, she signed me up with Alex Fevola's modelling agency in Frankston. People had been telling Mum for years that she should 'get Sharni into modelling', but that was more my sister's scene. Kara was the girly, pretty and popular one, not me. She loved clothes, make-up, dolls and shopping – basically, everything I loathed.

'Just give it a go,' Mum said. 'If you get a couple of jobs you can start saving for your own horse.'

Well played, Karin Layton. Well played.

So began my brief spell as a model. I did a couple of magazine shoots and shopping-centre catwalks. I even had an audition for *Neighbours* at one point, but I was a useless actress so that didn't go too well. Katie and I practised the lines together beforehand, which was way more fun than the actual audition. Turns out it's harder than it looks to pretend there's a bird in a room when there isn't. The whole time I was just thinking, *How do I say 'Oh look, there's a bird' when there's no bird?* I decided that acting wasn't made for the logically and pedantically minded. Namely, me.

But I stuck with the modelling for a couple more years, and when *Search for a Supermodel* came to Melbourne, the agency entered me. I was fourteen then, the lowest entry age, and Mum and I had to hang around Melbourne Arena for fifteen hours as I successfully made it through each round. Before I knew what was happening, I had made it into the top twenty finalists, which meant I had to dress myself for the final rounds. This is when the wheels began to fall off.

I had absolutely no idea what to wear (where was Kara when I needed her?) and no idea how to do my make-up, which was also expected of me. I looked to my mum for her wisdom and guidance, but her eyes clearly said, *Don't ask me, I've got no idea!* It was abundantly clear to everyone that I didn't belong in that world. Only the final twelve went through to the next stage, and I was one of the eight who missed out. The judges lined us (the losers) up to give us their feedback. 'Even the tallest models are only five-foot-eleven.'

Wow. I was even too tall for *modelling*? For God's sake! Was there anything tall girls could do in this world?

A lady from Vivien's Model Management gave me her card, but I was done. I waited until she'd walked away and then threw the card in a nearby bin.

'Take me back to my horses, Mum,' I begged.

My short-lived modelling career had come to an end, and I was fine with that. Despite my failure as a child model and insecurities about my height, not much bothered me then. I was a pretty chilled-out teenager, and Mum's friends would often comment on how mature I was for my age. I think this had a lot to do with my horses. They were always there when I was feeling low or needed a mane to cry on. I wasn't into 'teenage-girl dramas' and neither were my friends. Midway through high school, I was part of a group known as the 'Oddbotts', called so because we were a mix of personalities and types. I was into sport, Katie was into music, another girl was into boys, another was a surfy chick and the other a homebody. We were the safety-net group that girls came to when they didn't fit in anywhere else. Our group was a judgement-free zone and we never fought, which is what I loved the most about them. I didn't want a bar of anyone who was too cool, or too dramatic, and I had no interest in boys … until Year Nine.

My first boyfriend was the brother of a mate from the pony club. He was tall and super cute. I was also tall, and pretty cute, so we made a good match. Also, he'd seen me in my jodhpurs with no make-up on and knew what he was getting. I was never a girl who was going to pretend I was something I wasn't for a boy. The relationship was very similar to the one I'd had in Year Six. It was more about saying 'Yeah, she's my girlfriend/he's my boyfriend' in front of others than it was about us having actual feelings for each other. We went to the movies together, because that's what people who dated did; he came to my horse events, because that's what a boyfriend did; and I'd watch him play basketball, because that's what a girlfriend did. And on weekends, my friends and I would go to his house and drink Woodstocks with him and his mates while his parents were at the other end of the house.

After a few months I realised he was making more of an effort with his mates than he was with me, so I broke it off. I did it nicely, though. His family was awesome and I knew them well from the pony club, so I took flowers around to his mum and dad with a card to say thanks for putting up with me. Mum had always taught me to say thank you, even when I was dumping someone's son because he was annoying. After this, I decided my time was better spent playing netball, riding my horse and hanging out with my mates for a while. I wasn't interested in boys asking me out. I just wanted them to accept me as one of them.

It wasn't until Year Ten that I had my next short-lived romance – a cute eighteen-year-old who was just as immature as me. I only saw him on weekends because of my weekly netball commitments and school. Also, I wasn't comfortable staying over at his house, so I didn't, and my parents had a strict no-boys-at-sleepovers rule, which wasn't a problem with me. I never let myself feel pressured to sleep with guys if I didn't want to, which may have had something to do with the fact that I was six-foot-two and brimming with self-confidence (thanks Mum and Dad!). A friend of mine convinced me to break up with the cute eighteen-year-old, only to start dating him herself the following week (she clearly had chicks before dicks the wrong way around). I was upset but not heartbroken. After all, I had my friends, my sport and my horses to keep me distracted.

Katie's sixteenth birthday party came around, and in a show of parental leniency, her mum said we could drink two Vodka Cruisers each. Back then, drinking at parties was something every teenager in our area was doing. But most times the parents were around supervising us, so we always felt safe and never went overboard. Halfway through Katie's party, her mum dragged her inside.

'Katie, I said not much drinking tonight, and there's a beer bong outside!'

'Yeah, but it's only the boys who are doing it!'

'Then why is *Sharni* doing it?'

It was the first time I'd ever seen a beer bong, and since the boys were doing it, I wanted to give it a go. This sums up my attitude towards boys then. Whatever they could do, I could do better – including beer bongs.

Times you should apologise #23

When the maths teacher kicks you out of the classroom for chucking your best friend's pencil case out the window and distracting the entire class.

(SORRY, KATIE)

CHAPTER SEVEN

TALL GIRLS WELCOME HERE

Every Victorian netball-playing kid dreams of making the Stage League A team and playing on the courts at Royal Park. They're close to Melbourne CBD and the Royal Melbourne Zoo, and all the young guns in the State League teams play on their hallowed bitumen.

I had trialled for the Frankston Peninsula State League A teams many times as a youngster but was never good enough. The Under 13s and Under 15s B teams played on the less hallowed courts, far from the city, in Waverley.

Our Under 15s State League B team was a great side, and the competition wasn't as strong as it was at Royal Park, so we did really well. Playing with the B team also gave me a chance to flex my goal-shooting skills for the first (and only) time in my life. In the Under 15s Grand Final, we were struggling to score in the first half, so at half-time I switched from Goal Keeper to Goal Shooter and scored goal after goal (thanks to my height) and we won the game. It was so much fun playing in a stress-free environment. Once you've made the A team, in any age group, there's a lot of pressure to perform. Pressure on yourself, your parents and the clubs expectations.

For those unfamiliar with the way the divisions work in netball, Squad, where I was playing, is one level below State League, and this is where you can potentially be identified for State academies, which is where I was playing for Chelsea. At fifteen I was playing in the Chelsea Squad team, and having a great old time, when someone came along who would change the whole trajectory of my life and kickstart my netball career.

That someone was Stan. Stan the man.

No, Stan wasn't the next love of my life. He was a selector who took a chance on me when no-one else would. Stan had an eye for talent, and after watching me play one day, talent-identified me for the Victorian Pathways. This one act from Stan meant that I was finally eligible to try out for a state team, and it was a huge deal for me. So many other selectors and teams had turned a blind eye to me over the years, worried it would be too hard to get my long limbs under control, but Stan saw my potential. To this day I credit him with my rise to success in the netball world.

This experience also taught me a very important life lesson: your success in a chosen field can often come down to one person's opinion or decision. It's why I believe it's important to surround yourself with people who have faith in you. That's half the battle to succeeding.

Soon after Stan's momentous decision (for me, anyway) in 2003, I trialled for the Under 16s Victorian Schoolgirls team and got a spot. Suddenly, I was rocketed to a top-twelve player position in the Victorian Under 16s age group, my first real promotion in the netball world. I'd always been told I was 'too lanky' or 'too uncoordinated' at trial after trial. More often than not I would just get a call saying I didn't make the team and be given no explanation at all, which can be pretty soul-destroying for a teenage girl. So, making the Victorian Schoolgirls team meant the world to me, because I had been *seen*.

We trained at the Methodist Ladies' College campus and even travelled across the country to play a tournament in Perth. This was where I saw Chelsea Pitman play for the first time. Chelsea was a superstar of under-age netball in those days and still plays netball at the top level today. Of course, I had no idea back in 2003 that Chelsea and I would end up playing in the same team one day. That was still a long way off.

I was always so intimidated by girls who were 'netball prodigies'; the girls who played at Royal Park. I just didn't see myself as being on the same spectrum as them at all. On the Perth tournament, a daily newsletter was given out and someone wrote that I resembled Janine Ilitch, who was playing in the Australian team at the time. This should have been a huge ego boost, but I didn't know Janine, or any netballers for that matter (thanks mainstream media), so it didn't mean a thing to me.

'Sharni, you're doing so well!' Mum said. 'They say you play like Janine Ilitch!'

'Who's Janine Ilitch?'

Mum shrugged. 'I don't know, but she plays for Australia, so she must be good!'

'Thanks, Mum.'

Clearly Mum knew as many professional netballer names as I did.

I'd just returned home from the Perth Tournament when Mum came into my room one morning.

'Sharni, Jane Searle is on the phone for you.'

I frowned. 'Who's Jane Searle?'

'She said she coaches the Melbourne team, and it sounds important!'

What the ...?

My heart was pounding as I picked up the phone. 'Hello?'

'Hi Sharni, my name's Jane Searle,' a friendly voice said. 'I'm the coach of the Melbourne Kestrels and we want you to come on board as a training partner. We have sixteen spots and would like to give one to you. Would you be interested?'

Stunned pause.

'Sharni?'

'Yes, of course!'

'Okay, great, we'll see you at training this Saturday. Bye.'

'Um, okay, thanks, bye ...'

I hung up and turned to my waiting Mum.

'Holy shit! I'm training with the Melbourne team!'

Neither of us could believe this was actually happening. We had no idea how this woman even knew who I was! I later found out that Cathy Fellows, my Victorian coach from the Perth Tournament, was the Assistant Coach at the Melbourne Kestrels. She'd recommended me to Jane after I played underneath her at the Perth Tournament.

When I got picked in the Melbourne team, I went from being in the Under 15s B Peninsula Peninsula team to the Championship division, meaning I'd skipped about seven teams on the ranking system. This was an insanely fast rise to the top after all those years of never being selected. In one phone call, my entire world had done a one-eighty, and I had no idea just how much my life was about to change. I was required to be in the Championship team so I could play at a level that would get me up to speed with the Melbourne Team as quickly as possible.

I was pretty nervous on the drive to my first training session with the Melbourne Kestrels the following Saturday morning. Rightly so, as it turned out. Man, was that session a massive wake-up call.

I was completely out of my depth. Our trainer, Stoxy, was a hard-arse army dude, and when we arrived at the Melbourne Royal Botanic Gardens, he made all sixteen of us run around the perimeter of the gardens carrying a huge, heavy boat rope. It was 20 metres long, and any time we let any part of it touch the ground all of us had to do twenty push-ups. I got the fright of my life the first time Stoxy roared at us when the rope touched the ground.

'GET DOWN AND GIVE ME TWENTY!'

I was terrified. I couldn't do *one* push-up, let alone twenty! My skinny arms trembled beneath me as Stoxy stood over me and shouted, 'SHARNI, drop to your knees!'

Stoxy had obviously failed to notice that I *was* on my knees and *still* couldn't do a push-up!

The next week we travelled to the 1000 Steps Walk in the Dandenong Ranges, where Stoxy made us do an 800-metre run, followed by a sprint to the top of the steps. It nearly killed me, but I made it to the top and was feeling pretty chuffed as I turned to head back down to the bottom.

Faaaarrrrk, that was hard, I thought, joining the rest of my panting teammates. *Thank God it's over.*

'Okay, ladies!' Stoxy announced. 'Up we go again, but this time you need to do ten push-ups every one hundred steps!'

I wanted to die. And when I finally made it to the top, I seriously thought I was going to.

I was well and truly ready to wrap things up when I reached the bottom again, only to hear Stoxy say, 'Okay ladies, third time lucky! This time you have to piggyback each other up the stairs!'

I wasn't capable of getting myself back up there, let alone someone else, so my poor partner, Andy Booth, carried me the whole way up those steps. I clung to her, sobbing with exhaustion and embarrassment all the way up and back.

Those Kestrels sessions were BRUTAL. Never in my life had I trained like that, and to this day they are still the hardest I've done by far.

I'd felt on top of the world after Jane's phone call, assuming this was my big breakthrough and that I was on my way to the big netball league. But once I started training with the Kestrels, I soon realised that making it in the big league, or even getting the chance to step one foot on the court, was going to be *much* harder than I could have imagined. And I hadn't even started the Victorian Certificate of Education (VCE) yet.

A few weeks into January 2004, I took the big step into Year Eleven. It was the beginning of my final, and most important, years of high school and I'd never felt more exhausted. Taking on a new netball training regime – the likes of which I'd never experienced – was really knocking me about physically and mentally. I was growing new muscles, and training better each session, but I was completely knackered.

Still, it was a huge thrill rocking up to my first day of Year

Eleven and proudly announcing that I was now 'one of the girls who play for the Melbourne team'. Two girls from my school, Briony Cargill and Pia McGeoch, were also in the Melbourne teams. I'd always looked up to them as elite netballers and couldn't believe I was playing at the same level as them.

The Kestrels trained every weekday — two sessions before school and three after school each week. On Mondays, Wednesdays and Fridays we trained on court, and on Tuesdays and Thursdays we did weights in the gym. The weekends were for playing games.

Mum's joy at her daughter's netball promotion quickly turned to horror when she learned that I needed to be in Parkville (a fifty-minute drive from Bonbeach) at 5.30am two mornings a week during preseason. On these mornings I went to bed in my training clothes and socks the night before. The only thing I had to do in the morning was put my shoes on and grab my packed school bag. My poor mum had to wake me at 4.20am when I would roll out of bed and plonk myself in the car. It wasn't a routine that was too dissimilar to the Sunday-morning horse events, but now we were doing it twice a week, rather than once every few months.

After training, I'd hop back in the car and eat the breakfast Mum had bought me from the nearby Queen Victoria Market, while Mum drove me to school in time for my first class at 8am. If Mum had to work, Briony and I got the train back together, and when Briony got her licence, she drove me back. We'd stop at Macca's for bacon and egg McMuffins and hash browns on the way, the BEST treat after a hard training session!

After-school training sessions were pretty full-on, too. Mum would pick me up from school and take me straight to Parkville for the 6–8pm session. When we finally arrived home at 9pm, I'd eat dinner and fall into bed around 10pm, before having to get up early the next day to get down to the paddocks and feed the horses before school. Juggling the Melbourne team, the State League team and the Under 17s Victorian team commitments, along with horseriding and VCE, meant that life was pretty hectic.

This was a crazy schedule for a sixteen-year-old, but I was lucky to have supportive parents, especially my mum/full-time driver. Mum and Dad knew how much I loved sport. They also knew that not many kids from our area got the opportunity to train with a Melbourne team like the Kestrels. When he was eighteen, Dad had been invited to train with the Melbourne Football Club but had no way of making it to training on time after work. He missed out on his one shot to play in the AFL and didn't want me to have to miss out, too. Mum felt the same way and understood that my mad schedule and early mornings were part of training to be an elite athlete. Like so many other professional athletes, I wouldn't have been able to do anything in those early years without Mum driving me around and picking me up. She made sure I got to every training session and let me sleep on those drives to get in some extra rest.

Mum also knew that I was a kid who needed to be plugged into a schedule like this to use up all my excess energy, strength and focus. But I definitely wasn't self-motivated at sixteen, and it was only thanks to Mum that I made those training sessions at all. She'd literally drag my arse out of bed on cold mornings. Funnily enough, I was always happy to get up early and go down to ride my horse!

Balancing my new netball training regime with school was

tough, but with Mum's support and Dad's lessons on goal setting, priorities and time management, I developed the skills to make it work. I had the perfect combination of parents – The Carer and The Motivator – and they were definitely the ones who set me up for success.

I decided to take on two Year Twelve subjects in Year Eleven, which would help lighten the load in my final year. My teammate, Mel Kitchin, was a huge inspiration in this area, too. She was in the year above me, completing Year Twelve, and whenever we travelled, she always had her head in her books. No wonder she got over 99 on her ENTER score. Yes, Mel is smart, but my oath did she work for it!

Even though I was in Year Eleven I was still acting the smart-arse and slacking off in the subjects I found hard. Chemistry was the hardest. At the start of most lessons, I'd tell the teacher I had to go to the toilet, then leave school and walk across the road to get something to eat. I'd arrive back in class just as the bell was ringing for the next period, so it's little wonder I had no clue what the teacher was talking about when I was there.

Since then, I've wondered if the reason I gave up so quickly on difficult subjects was that sport always came so easily. All those years of winning sporting trophies and awards made it harder to accept that I was average or 'slow' at anything. It was just easier to give up on the hard stuff. Now I know that the pay-off is far more rewarding when you *do* put in the work with the hard stuff. When you start improving at something you initially found challenging, it's a huge rush.

Ah, hindsight. So clear, yet so completely useless.

Mum supported me 100 per cent with my schoolwork, and

was impressed with the way I was managing everything, too. At parent–teacher night that year, my English teacher frowned across the table at us and said, 'Look, Karin. Sharni is doing way too much and she needs to give something up.'

Mum liked being told how to parent as much as I liked getting up at 4am to train. Without knowing it, my teacher had set off a Kaz trigger.

'Well,' Mum said, 'I guess she'd better give up school then.'

My teacher just stared as Mum got up and walked out. I jumped up to follow her, trying hard not to high-five my sassy mother and yell, 'BURN!' at my stunned teacher.

Definitely one of my all-time fave 'Mum Moments'.

Mum wasn't a pushy parent, so I think it irked her when my teacher said I was doing too much. Mum always encouraged me, but she never forced any decisions on me. She knew I had a lot on my plate, but she also knew the opportunities I had in front of me, and she wasn't going to let a judgey comment stand in my way. More than anyone, Mum understood how happy my horses made me and that taking my riding away would only cause me more stress. I was lucky to have a mum who knew what I needed, and what was best for me. And this teacher just thought she was saying the right thing because English was my best subject and she had high expectations of me. (PS Miss Wolf – I'm writing a book!)

I met James a few months into Year Eleven. He went to the boys' school near Mentone Girls' Secondary and we had mutual mates. We met at a party and I wasn't interested at first, but the dude was persistent and I finally agreed to a Timezone-and-movies date.

On our first date we played a bunch of games in the arcade and won ourselves plastic water pistols and bouncy balls. When the movie finished the two of us spent a couple of hours running all over the deserted shopping centre, biffing balls and shooting water at each other. *This is my kind of guy*, I thought, and soon afterwards – and for the first time in my short life – I realised I might actually like this guy.

Kara's knowledge of all things girly finally came in handy when she became my fashion consultant, and hair and make-up artist on date nights with my new boyfriend. That was if I could be bothered getting out of my jodhpurs and Blink-182 hoodies.

I wasn't the typical lovey-dovey type teenager, though, and I absolutely hated public displays of affection. But despite my fear and loathing of all things 'mushy', I fell for James in a big way, even though I was training so much that I didn't get to see him as much as I would have liked.

There were sixteen of us in the Kestrels team, but only twelve of us were chosen for the weekly games. If I wanted to play in those games, I had to work my arse off to make Jane and the other coaches believe I was a Goal Keeper worth putting on that court. When I first started training, I could barely keep up with the skills and speed of the other girls. They had been playing top-level netball week in and week out for years, so they were way ahead of me. I always felt like I slowed the drills down at training. I'd watch as the ball flew past my face and spun around my head, and would feel completely uncoordinated alongside my much better teammates. But they were always supportive of me, and a few of the older girls, like Melinda Cranston, Chelsea Nash and Amanda Burton, really took me under their wings. I also made friends with the girls my age like Madi Browne, Caity Thwaites, Mel Kitchin, Amy Steele and Shae Brown (nee Bolton). I loved being on the team with the younger girls as they made it feel a bit less intimidating and scary.

Being younger also meant we could be pretty immature at times. Amy and I liked to muck around at training. During passing drills we'd pair up and throw the ball as hard as we could at each other's heads or knees, then crack up laughing when the other didn't catch it. We were eventually banned from partnering up during passing drills, or any other activity that involved pairs … or balls. That kind of behaviour 'wasn't acceptable' when training in a high-performance environment. Although we were on the path to becoming elite athletes, Amy and I were still so young and didn't always see it that way. We still had one foot in the serious high-performance sport camp, and one in the naughty teenage-girl camp. I've never taken my foot completely out of the latter camp. I don't think Amy has either.

Amy, Shae and I were still playing in the State League on Wednesday nights to get game time. This was because we weren't getting games with the Kestrels on weekends. The three of us would train for two hours with the Kestrels, then each eat an entire pizza before playing a State League game forty minutes later. We soon realised that forty minutes isn't enough time to digest one slice of pizza, let alone a whole one. We had fun, though.

Spending my entire first year with the Kestrels not playing a single game, however, was *not* fun. I knew this was part of the deal for any young player picked up by the team, but it still sucked. Training is the hardest part, and I was doing it non-stop without getting the pay-off of playing an actual game.

Mum and I went to watch the Australian netball team that year and all I could think while watching them play was, *I can't make the top twelve in my current team! How the hell will I ever make the top twelve in the country?!*

A year after starting with the Kestrels, I had zero faith in myself or my ability, and truly believed I had no chance of ever getting where I wanted to be.

Times you should apologise #19

When you convince your friend to start a petition
to change the Year Twelve song because it sucks, and she gets in
trouble for it.
(SORRY, BEC)

CHAPTER EIGHT

BALANCING ACT

When 2005 began, I decided to punch out this final year of high school in true 'Sharni Getting Shit Done' style. Taking things slowly had never been my thing, which was handy since Year Twelve was going to be a full-throttle year.

I'd completed two Year Twelve subjects in Year Eleven, which meant I only had to concentrate on four, rather than five, subjects. I figured that I could manage the study load if I used my free periods and lunchtimes effectively. This was crucial since I was now playing in three different netball teams and didn't have time to study after school.

Three nights a week I trained with the Melbourne Kestrels, then I trained and played with my State League team twice a week, and had a three-hour training session with the Victorian Under 17s team every Sunday. When you add travel time on top of all that, there wasn't much time left over for studying ... or anything else, really. I would see Katie and my other friends at school, but I was lucky to see James once a week, if at all.

Often, I'd train for fifteen days straight without a break. Then

I'd have one day off and do another fifteen to twenty days straight again. It was wild and I was constantly tired. I knew I wasn't the only player with this crazy schedule, which helped me to suck it up and get on with it. There were at least five of us in the same age group who were all completing high school and training in these teams. Unfortunately, athlete management wasn't a focus or priority back then. The coach of each team wanted all of us there, *all* the time and they did a pretty poor job of communicating with each other. Priorities were always around what was best for the team, not what was best for us as individual athletes, and a lot of young netballers ended up with shin splints caused by over-training.

If the coaches had better communication, they could have worked out a roster between themselves where we'd have at least one day off a week. This would give our bodies and minds a chance to recover. For example, I might miss a Kestrels' training one week and a State League training the next, then a State Team training the week after that. But that was a system that simply didn't exist.

'We know you've had a busy week,' our coaches would say, 'but you still have to train, so just train at 60 per cent.'

Okay, Coach, I'd think to myself. *So, if I'm in a drill and everyone else is going at 100 per cent, how am I meant to jog and go at half-pace?*

We couldn't and we didn't. We just trained all the time at 100 per cent. None of us wanted to run the risk of not being picked for a team because we weren't training to the best of our ability, so we learned how to run on empty.

This kind of schedule affected each of us in different ways

as training seven days a week takes a toll on you physically and mentally. For the younger ones in the teams, our bodies were still growing, so we were constantly pulling up with soft-tissue injuries, usually our hip flexors, glutes or quadriceps. Other girls ended up with more serious injuries, like shin splints or torn anterior cruciate ligaments (ACLs) due to over-training. There is a high rate of torn ACLs that occur while a woman is menstruating since our ligaments stretch during our periods and put us at higher risk of injury. This is why it's so important for females who play sport to know their cycles, so they can keep track of when they're at a higher risk of injuring themselves.

My dream of playing in the World Youth Cup kept me going during this time. When I made the Australian Under 17s squad, we headed off for a camp in Canberra and I was starstruck to be training with netball's revered open-age Australia Coach, Norma Plummer. For those who aren't familiar with the famously tough lady of Australian netball, picture Meryl Streep's character in *The Devil Wears Prada*. Norma has the hair, the fashion and the attitude to match.

We arrived at the Canberra camp and were standing around in the auditorium when Norma marched in. The 21/U Australian team had just lost to New Zealand in the Netball World Youth Cup in Florida. Though Norma was no longer the 21/U coach herself at the time, I knew she prided herself on being the coach of the best netball-playing country in the world. She did *not* like losing, even indirectly.

'Ladies,' she said loudly, 'the current Australian World Youth Cup team has just lost, and the next World Youth Cup is in four years' time.'

Her steely green eyes scanned each one of us. I was sure she could see my knees shaking.

'*You* will be the age group that gets selected to go,' she said, pointing a finger at us, 'and when you do, YOU WILL NOT LOSE!'

I barely knew this lady, but she scared the absolute shit out of me and that day I knew what I wanted more than anything. To play in that World Youth Cup, and to win.

When I got back to Melbourne after the camp, I was so exhausted that I struggled to maintain concentration in classes. It would be tough on any elite athlete in Year Twelve to complete more than four subjects, so I felt relieved that I'd made that decision. There was no way my mind would have allowed me to take in any more information than it already was. I was running at maximum mental capacity.

Injuries are always more likely to happen when you're mentally strained because you have neural fatigue. Your brain is sending messages to your body parts much more slowly than usual, so you don't react as quickly if you turn or land the wrong way. BANG! Instant twelve-month injury.

They are many ways of testing for this type of neural fatigue now, but no-one was testing us in 2005. It was 'power on' mode twenty-four seven. At least, that's how it felt.

Our second preseason camp to Traralgon, however, was still a massive shock to my system. We were woken every night at two or three o'clock in the morning to go dirt running and do five-minute planks. If anyone dropped, we'd have to start again. Time and again those sessions challenged me, but I also found a strength I didn't know I possessed to keep going.

I had no idea how hard I was able to push myself before the Kestrels' training sessions with Stoxy came into my life. I'd always believed that if I pushed myself too hard physically something bad could happen, but the mental training soon helped me break through those boundaries. Internal fears and thoughts like, *There's no way I can get through another session*, were slowly being stamped out of me every week. When I'd had to climb those stairs on that first training session, I truly believed I couldn't do it. But with encouragement from my teammates and Stoxy, I kept putting one foot in front of the other and got it done. Just by completing that one difficult challenge, I started breaking down the mental barriers I'd had in place and *believing* I could do it, which was a huge breakthrough.

I wasn't aware of it at the time, but I was starting to create positive experiences for my mental piggy bank. These experiences would go towards strengthening my belief in myself over time. When we had to hold a plank position for five minutes, I never wanted to drop because I didn't want to be the one to let everyone down. I was learning that training in a group is far more motivating for me than training alone. I was externally, not internally, motivated.

Individual athletes are internally motivated. They can make themselves get out of bed to train alone. But most team-sport players are externally motivated. We are inspired to keep going by those around us. Neither is right or wrong – you are who you are. But I was most definitely externally motivated. Having a team to spur me on was the best thing for my mental and physical health. I was driven by the amazing and inspiring women around me, and I would keep my knees off the ground, determined not to add one extra minute to the plank, no matter how much pain I was in. And I was in a lot of pain! I was so proud of myself when it was over and added another positive experience to my mental piggy bank.

A few negative experiences found their way into the mental piggy bank, too. Like the fact that I only played three games during my second season with the Kestrels. The first one was against Newcastle and it was tough. We were down by fifteen points and I remember sitting on the bench thinking, *Please don't put me on!* As much as you train to play, when you're going on for the very first time you are scared shitless! An outsider might assume you'd be chomping at the bit to get on the court after all that training, but the first game for any athlete is so daunting. I'd been training so hard and for so long for a moment that had finally arrived. Yet, all I could hear when the coach called my name at half-time and threw a GK bib at me was the terrified screaming inside my head.

I didn't have much of an impact (if any) in my first-ever Kestrels game and we ended up losing by twenty goals. But I could finally say that I had my first game under my belt, and my teammates all gave me a big hug to celebrate the occasion. All I could think was, *Thank God that's out of the way!*

A few weeks later, we played the Queensland Firebirds. Jane put me on for the second half of the game again and I played a bit better this time, having gotten the first-game jitters out of my system. I liked playing interstate games, too. It was televised on the ABC but didn't have a huge audience so there wasn't as much pressure for me personally as when I was playing at home with friends and family watching. We won the Firebirds game and

I'd managed to intercept a few passes so I was happy with my performance and relieved that I hadn't embarrassed myself.

I wouldn't be so lucky the third time around.

The New South Wales Swifts were at the top of the ladder, and even though I really wanted to play, I also really wanted to stay on the bench in my comfort zone. At least for the first quarter or two. In my first two games with the Kestrels I hadn't gone on the court until halfway through the match, which is easier than going on in the first half, especially for a rookie like me. You could sit on the bench and watch your likely opponent (Goal Attack or Goal Shooter for me) closely, to observe what your teammates were or weren't doing well. By the time you get on the court, you know exactly what your game plan is.

On this day, Jane told me I'd be starting as Goal Keeper, five minutes before the start of our game against the top team. I was truly terrified. I'd be playing against Australia's best shooter, Cath Cox, so it would have been nice to have a bloody heads-up!

The team selection process on game day in netball is so random. You only find out if and where you are playing five minutes before heading onto the court. The thinking behind this strategy is that you are always physically and mentally geared up to play at any moment. This is fine for an experienced player who's been around the block, but terrible for a seventeen-year-old who is new to elite sport. I didn't yet know about the practice of analysing your opposition players in the week before the game. I'd eventually learn that this is a huge part of being a proactive player and knowing what to do when you come up against your opponent, rather than being reactive and waiting until you're on court before you figure out their game. A reactive game rarely works out well, as was proven during this, my third game, with the Kestrels.

When Jane threw that bib at me, I panicked. I hadn't started a game *ever*. Why this one Jane, *why?* I had zero confidence and the negative self-talk began.

I can't play netball ... last week was a fluke!

One good game of netball didn't provide nearly enough positive experience coins for the mental piggy bank. I'd be playing against Australia's best shooter and knew this was one of those make-or-break moments. The other giant worry was that I wouldn't be hiding in an interstate match. This game was on my home turf, at Melbourne Arena, in front of six thousand people. The biggest crowd I'd ever played in front of. It was a double-header, two games in one night, with the other Melbourne team. We were usually lucky to get a couple of hundred people along to a game, so numbers like this weren't the norm for us and it was overwhelming. A coach I had later in my career always told us how many people were in the crowd. She did this so we could prepare ourselves before walking out as she believed that having the fewest possible unknowns in your head helps you focus on the job at hand and not get distracted before a game.

No such luck this night. Not only was I freaked out and distracted by the massive crowd, but also by my family, who was there, too. Mum and Dad always came along to my games, whether I was playing or not, but I would finally be starting in a big game. I was so worried I'd embarrass myself in front of them both, especially Mum. I was thinking about all those hours she'd spent in the car, driving me to and from training sessions, and all the sacrifices she'd made to support me in this sport. I wanted to prove that it was all worth it. That I was good enough to be here, playing at Melbourne Arena. That it hadn't been a waste of her time. These negative thoughts were all-consuming and left no space for the tactical part of my brain to do what it needed to.

From the moment my name was called, my legs turned to lead and my eyes grew heavy. I had completely psyched myself out, and I got smashed as a result. Cath Cox easily ripped me a new one and I was dragged at quarter time.

When humans are stressed, we can only take in one or two pieces of information at a time. I know now that if I'd just asked the coach to give me two things to focus on it would have kept my mind on task, and not allowed the negative thoughts to creep in. But I didn't know that then, which is why I talked myself out of the game before it even started.

Jane took me off at the end of the first quarter and I was gutted. I wanted to quit there and then and couldn't even bring myself to look up at my mum and dad. I buried my head in my hands, too ashamed to see the disappointment on their faces. When I finally did look up towards them, I instantly saw the pained, sympathetic look on Mum's face and had to look away before I burst into tears. I continued watching the game but didn't take anything in. The Swifts were too far ahead for us to win, and it was my fault. By allowing them to get so many goals in the first quarter, I'd let the team down.

There's a saying, 'What you believe, you will conceive,' and it was true of me and the way I played that day. I didn't prepare myself mentally for the game and so I flopped when given a great opportunity. I'd trained so hard, waiting for my moment in the sun, but instead of grabbing it when it finally came, I threw it away.

I overthought every moment on that court and you just don't have time to do that in netball. It's a fast game and you have three seconds to make a decision. If you spend too long thinking about where you're going to throw the ball, or how you're going to get it off the other team, you've missed your chance. That happened time and time again in my first, and only, quarter of that game. The best athletes trust in their training and allow their instincts to take over on game day. But at that early stage of my career, instead of being in the game and playing in the moment, I was just thinking, *I can't believe I missed that ball! Idiot!* and *C'mon Layton! You didn't even run with her!*

These thoughts are hugely unhelpful when you're trying to get yourself back on task. Let's say you're cooking a lasagne. You start well, constructing this perfect layered creation and putting it in the oven, but when it's time to pull it out you just stare at it and think, 'Come on, just take it out!' And then it burns. You know what you're meant to do, but you're so busy yelling at yourself for not doing it that it all goes wrong and you end up with a black charred mess, which is pretty much how I felt after the game.

I thought Jane would give me feedback afterwards, even if it was all negative, but she didn't say a word to me. No words. Nothing. This instantly made me think my performance was so woeful that it wasn't worth mentioning ever again. I'd disappointed her so deeply that she couldn't even look at or talk to me.

The following week I was dropped from the twelve and put back in the sixteen, and with that, any skerrick of confidence I possessed went sailing out the window. A few weeks went by with no communication from any of the coaching staff. No eye contact at training or feedback of any kind, good or bad. Could I have asked for feedback? Probably. But this was a 'do as you're told and stay quiet' era of netball for young ones like me. The rookie always carried the balls to training and was known as the shitkicker (endearingly), so being at the bottom of the food chain didn't exactly inspire me to speak up. I didn't think I had the right to ask about, or question, the coach's decisions. I was the new kid on the block and I was all about following orders – at that young age, anyway!

I also didn't ask because I don't think I wanted to hear the answer. I didn't have the guts. A big part was the embarrassment of knowing I'd failed. My coaches and team knew I'd failed, too, so maybe everyone felt it was better to leave me alone. I now know that these difficult conversations are the ones that help you grow and learn. They're hugely important. But back then I was a kid who needed reassuring and didn't want to hear ugly truths about my flaws. The difference was that I was now in the world of elite sportspeople, so I'd have to learn to deal with it. And fast.

As I wasn't talking these things through with anyone, I just continued to have a whole lot of negative conversations with myself. This torment of *You're not good enough, Why are you even showing up to training? You're shit*, self-talk was manifesting itself in my training. The louder my inner voice got, the more I didn't want to be there. I didn't want to play this stupid game, and I eventually stopped trying, because why would I? I couldn't play for shit and was just embarrassing myself.

Seven weeks after that woeful game and halfway into the season, the Kestrels sent me back to State League training. They could see that I was on a downward spiral and they wanted to help me get my confidence back.

'Sharni, what's up with you?'

Kristy Keppich-Birrell, my State League coach, could see something was wrong the moment I walked through the door.

'I hate netball,' I said. 'I'm shit and I don't want to be here.'

Then Kristy did something I wasn't expecting. She smiled.

'Sharni, you played against Australia's best shooter,' she said. 'In your first game starting. And she kicked your arse. You should be happy that Cath Cox kicked your arse. What a great experience to learn from!'

I didn't know what to say. I'd never looked at it that way.

'How about you come back and play with us for a while?' she said. 'You'll soon realise how good you are compared to girls your own age, as opposed to Australia's best shooters.'

That conversation with Kristy changed my life, and my career. I went back to playing State League and, because I was going at my own pace for the first time in a while, loved it.

This period away from the Kestrels training sessions also meant that I had time on my hands to do the kind of stuff other girls my age were doing for the first time in ages. I was still young, yet life had gotten so serious so quickly and I hadn't really taken stock of all that had happened. I'd gone from being a fifteen-year-old playing netball just for fun, hanging out with my mates on a weekend and riding my horse, to a sixteen-year-old in a top state team with endless training sessions and no time for a social life or my horses – all within a few months.

I had been living like a full-time athlete, although this only pertained to how often I trained, not to how much I earned – a measly $1000 a year. It felt like I was constantly treading water. But when I was with James and my friends, it was different. I was free. I was happy. I could be myself.

James accepted me for who I was, and I had been desperately missing hanging out with him, and my friends. They would always text me when I was away with the Kestrels, saying how much they missed me and wished I was there. Even if I was home, I couldn't party with them because I always had a game the next day.

My friends didn't entirely understand what it meant to play sport at a top level and would sometimes try to pressure me into staying out late or drinking with them. I was conflicted because I missed them, but also felt so grateful for the amazing opportunity I'd been given. But, at the end of the day, I was still a kid, and all I really wanted was to hang out with my friends.

And now that I wasn't part of the Kestrels top twelve, that's exactly what I could do. I could be a normal teenager again. I only had to play State League games on Wednesday nights, so I was going to make the most of my newfound freedom. I decided to take Kristy's advice about playing netball with girls my age to feel more like them again and apply it to all areas of my life. In other words: it was my last few months of high school and I was going to have some fun.

My friends and I mostly went to house parties or on one of the local and very popular party buses on the weekends. Come Saturday night, one of the older guys would buy the drinks and we would jump on the party bus, drink and dance the night away. The bus would drop us off at Crown Casino in the city. Once there, those over eighteen would head to the pub, and the rest of us would run around Galactic Circus, grab some Maccas then get back on the bus for the drive home – standard teenage behaviour when I was growing up!

It was so much fun just being a normal teenager again, being rebellious but not doing anything stupid that would get me in too much trouble. The netball season was all over by September, which left me with a lot more time to study for my final Year Twelve exams. Once October hit and the looming VCE exams were becoming all too real, we put our partying aside to knuckle down and study. There'd be more than enough time for partying once school was done and dusted.

Up until Year Twelve I'd been considering quitting school to become a cabinet-maker and had studied woodwork all through school. But James and Mum insisted I give university a crack. The animal science degree had an ENTER score requirement of 72.15, and they knew I had the potential to get in.

I spent every recess and lunchtime studying maths with my teacher, doing extra lectures outside school and working with a tutor to get my grades back on track. As our exams got closer, James and I attended any and every exam lecture going and hit the books every night of the week.

I was quite nervous by the time exams came around. I'd tried so hard to lift my grades after years of dragging my feet, and I hoped all my hard work had been worth it. I'd never really cared about test results before Year Twelve, and I was terrified that I might have left it too late.

When the VCE results came out I was too scared to look, so Mum took the newspaper and started to search for my name. I felt like vomiting as she scanned the names and results.

'What score did you need to get into animal science?'

'72.15.'

Mum paused. 'Well, guess what? You got 72.15.'

HOLY SHIT. I grabbed the paper to see for myself, and there it was. Sharni Layton – 72.15. The *exact* score I'd been trying to achieve!

It was the first time in my life that I truly recognised and understood the power of goal-setting and manifestation. I mean, seriously, what were the odds of getting *exactly* what I'd been aiming for? But it would take a bit longer for me to figure out how to use the same power in other areas of my life.

I celebrated my results with James, Katie and our mates. I was on top of the world, but James was furious. Although he'd received a better score than me overall, I'd beaten him in maths, and he was the one who'd been tutoring me in it for the past six months. As for Katie, she was always a smart and well-disciplined student, so she got the marks she needed to get into her chosen university course in events management. Katie had been volunteering at Lunatic Entertainment ever since she'd done her work experience there in Year Ten. Over the past couple of years, she'd been inching closer to her dream job in live music events, and I was still tagging along with her to every gig I could make. (Quick sidetrack: Katie ended up living her dream! Over the years she's been the General Manager of Lunatic Entertainment and the St Jerome's Laneway Festival, and worked with acts like The Temper Trap and Gotye. She's now General Manager of the Victorian Music Development Office. Yeah, she's pretty awesome!)

James and I went our separate ways for schoolies. He headed off to Byron Bay with the boys, and I travelled to the Gold Coast with the girls. Soon after our respective holidays, we started drifting apart. Without our single shared focus of studying for school, we found that we had less in common and weren't enjoying each other's company anymore. James wanted to go to Camp America in the new year, so he was the one who made the call to pull the pin. I was heartbroken. James was my first love and it had taken a lot for me to open up to someone. I moped around for months and Mum even bought me a kitten to try and cheer me up. We named him Harvey and he is still with Mum today. Longest 'feel better' gift ever.

That summer, I got a call from Netball Australia telling me I'd been selected for the Australian Under 21s Squad. This news should have been exciting, but instead I just felt that familiar tightening in my chest.

The roller-coaster of netball was about to start up again.

CHAPTER NINE

IT'S NOT ASTHMA

I went on my very first Australian Under 21s Squad camp in January 2006 with our coach, Lisa Alexander, and twenty other girls, including my Kestrels mate, Amy. When we started running through our drills on the first day, something happened that was new to Sharni the Netballer but familiar to Sharni the Person.

I couldn't breathe.

As we did rep after rep, with Lisa shouting from the sidelines, I tried taking big gulps of air, but it wasn't working. The more I tried to get air into my lungs, the harder it became to breathe. Finally, I stopped running, gasping for air, and bent over. What was happening? Was this an asthma attack? I was light-headed, my eyes were watering, and little black dots started to enter my vision. I wanted to scream, but all I could manage was a broken *'I ... can't ... breathe!'*

The physio ran over to me.

'Lean your arms on your knees,' he said. 'Just relax your chest and breathe into your belly.'

Gassssp!

'It's okay, you're okay, breathe into your belly.'

Gradually, I started taking more air in and began breathing normally. I looked up to find everyone watching me. I'd caused a scene and it was embarrassing. Great. The 'Young Girl' on the squad is now the 'Girl Who Can't Breathe'. Bloody brilliant.

I started jogging again, trying to shake it off and get back to normal, but the uneasy feeling stayed with me. *What was that? What is wrong with me?* I wondered as I ran through the drills.

I managed to make it through the rest of the camp but had a couple more similar attacks. Whenever they came on, I had to stop and rest, which was annoying and embarrassing. After the camp, I went to see a doctor who told me I might have developed exercise-induced asthma. He gave me a puffer and I started taking it to every training session and game. I needed to be prepared as there was going to be a lot of netball training and games coming up with my third year with the Kestrels starting.

I was also beginning my first semester at the University of Melbourne. I loved animals more than anything in the world, especially horses, and I planned on completing the three-year animal science degree before getting my honours in horse studies. After that, I'd see where it led me. (The degree ... not the horses.)

Walking onto the University of Melbourne campus for the first time was pretty daunting. The place was huge and I was overwhelmed to think that I had actually gotten into this world-renowned institution. I felt like pinching myself as I stood in a line with dozens of others to fill out my HECS form and pick my subjects. When they asked if I wanted to study full-time or part-time, I know now that the smart answer, considering my sporting commitments, would have been 'part-time'. But I was cocky. *Hey*, I thought, *I got through VCE, so I'll be fine!* Plus, the thought of studying part-time for eight years scared the bejesus out of me. *Eight* years until I graduated? I'd be so *old*! (spoiler alert: I'm facepalming myself now, fifteen years later, still with no university degree).

So, I signed up for the full-time course. Most of my friends were studying a bachelor of arts and the like, and only had twelve contact hours a week, which left them with plenty of free time to work and play. I assumed my life would be similar once I was at university. But when I received my schedule, I saw that a science degree involved a twenty-five-hour contact week.

My normal day looked like this:

5.30am – wake up

6.15am – arrive at the train station for the 6.30am train

7.30am – arrive in the city

7.45am – arrive at uni

8am – start my first class

4pm – finish uni and walk to the tram stop

5pm – arrive at Kestrels training

6pm – start training

8pm – finish training

9.30pm – arrive home, shower, eat

10–10.30pm – bed.

Then I'd get up and do it all again the next day.

At this stage I had my licence (Mum was even more excited about this than me) but it was easier and cheaper to get the train into the city rather than deal with the stress of finding a park every day.

I met some great people in that first semester at uni and became friends with a girl named Marissa, or Maz for short. In

NO APOLOGIES

May, we headed to Werribee Zoo for an excursion to study specific animals' physiology and behaviour. Maz and I chatted as we took notes and watched the lions loll about.

'I volunteered with lions in South Africa once,' Maz said.

I gasped. 'WHAT?'

She went on to say that she and her friends were going to Thailand to volunteer with elephants at the end of the year, and I couldn't believe what I was hearing. Was this actually a thing a person could do? That would be my absolute dream!

'Wanna come along?' Maz asked, reading my mind.

'Um … YES!' I squealed. 'I'd love to!'

During 'research' time in the library the next day, Maz and I booked our stay at the Elephant Nature Park in Thailand, with a plan to leave on Boxing Day and return six weeks later. I was so excited. It was nice to have something to look forward to, especially when I wasn't particularly happy with the way my life was going at that point, almost halfway through the year.

I thought I'd be able to cope with the study load in my degree, but I was SO wrong. My expectations were vastly different from the reality of the situation, and it hit me hard. The course was tough, made tougher because I'd ditched chemistry in Year Eleven and I didn't understand a lot of my lectures. It was a wake-up call when I realised that while I considered myself smart, I wasn't 'book smart' and study didn't come easily to me. If I wanted to keep up with my uni course, I'd have to put as much time into learning how to study as I did into my training. Unfortunately, I was training so much that I had little time left for books.

I couldn't understand how I had gone through twelve years of education and yet had no idea how to write an essay at a university

77

standard. There was zero similarity between the way I'd studied at school and the way I needed to study at university. I'd had so much help in VCE but now I was left to my own devices, and this was not how I worked best. I was an externally motivated kind of girl. I couldn't understand why my VCE teachers would spoonfeed us when that wasn't preparing us for tertiary education. Teaching styles may be different these days, but I certainly didn't feel prepared for university back then.

My university lecturers were great and very understanding. They knew how stretched I was for time, and were doing their best to help me between lectures, but it wasn't enough. I had worked my tail off to get the score I got in Year Twelve maths, which was Fundamentals of Mathematics – the easier maths. At university I was expected to know and understand Mathematical Methods – the harder maths – and I had absolutely no clue what I was doing.

It was a shit time all around.

I was emotional, exhausted, training poorly with the Melbourne Kestrels and my asthma attacks were getting worse. It was rare for me to get through a whole training session without pulling out at some point because I couldn't get enough oxygen into my lungs. The feeling of not being able to breathe was scary. These frequent attacks also meant that the coach wasn't putting me on in games, which was partly my fault, too, as my attitude during this time wasn't the greatest.

I can be a grumpy cow when I'm tired, and I'm sure the vibes I was giving to my coach were, 'I don't care if I don't play. Don't talk to me,' instead of 'Pick me, pick me!' which is what coaches want to see from their young players. But I was just too tired to care. I knew my coach expected me to give 100 per cent and to be grateful to be part of the team, but all I could think was, *Maybe I'd be more grateful if I wasn't training seven days a week!*

I'd been training with the Kestrels for three years and had only played a total of four games. I was a six-foot-two sixteen-year-old who weighed 62 kilograms when I first started with them. Within a year I weighed 70 kilograms, and two years in, I was up to 75 kilograms, and the extra weight was all muscle. That skinny, weak girl who struggled to do a single push-up at the Botanic Gardens was a distant memory, but all the extra muscle wasn't helping me get onto the court.

As the weeks and months passed, it became clear that I wouldn't be playing many games with the Kestrels that year, if any. Every week I'd spend yet another game on the bench and I was starting to wonder why I was training fourteen days straight without a break.

Being forced to watch your teammates play from the sidelines week after week is a shitty feeling, and it started having a negative effect on my self-esteem and confidence. I didn't feel like a true netty head, not like the other girls, and began to think I never would be. I was still training my heart out at every session, but it didn't seem to make a difference. I couldn't get on that court for love or money.

Some of my Victorian teammates had been picked up for professional teams when they turned eighteen. Their parents would tell Mum how excited their girls were but Mum had lost any excitement she'd once had about me being in the team. She saw the toll it had taken on me physically and mentally, and knew that my love of playing netball had died. Mum wanted me to enjoy my life, and she thought it was unfair for a kid so young to have been picked for the team only to be trained into the ground.

I'd been so pumped at my quick and unexpected rise to the top more than two years before, but now I wished I'd been left alone for another year or two. This would have given me the chance to mature more and therefore cope better with the professional sporting environment. As it was, by the time I did start to mature I was completely worn-out and obliterated.

It was over halfway through the netball season and I still hadn't played a single game with the Kestrels. I was well and truly over it. The whole season had been a balancing act with university and netball training, and it had all been a bit of a blur. Then I found out that I had failed three of my four university subjects in my first semester – this was the last straw. I needed to make a change.

I had a $4000 HECS fee from my first semester of uni, only for me to fail. If I went into Semester Two of my course I would already be behind financially, and I would most likely struggle again and possibly fail. I think I was so money-conscious because Mum and Dad had always worked so hard to give Kara and me the lives we had. I didn't know if I was going to commit myself to this course or not, and I didn't want to chuck thousands of dollars down the drain if it wasn't the direction I was going to go.

I deferred my course, hoping that a six-month break from study would have me feeling refreshed and energised for the following year. I might even go part-time like I should have in the first place. Ah, hindsight, there you are again.

Leaving uni halfway through the year meant I wouldn't see my future travelling companion, Maz, for six months before going to Thailand together, but that didn't really bother me. I knew we'd still get on when the time came.

It was looking unlikely that I'd get a game before the netball season wrapped up, but I could still try and improve before next season came around. Despite the hard year I'd had, I wasn't ready to give up on netball just yet.

I was still living at home, so Mum gave me a stern talk about getting a job since I was eighteen now. I agreed. I wanted to start doing my share and contributing to the family, too. I needed to make money and focus on getting my energy levels back up.

I called cafes, shops, cinemas and other local places but had no luck. No-one was keen to hire an eighteen-year-old with no work experience. Shock horror!

Then a friend said, 'Hey, have you thought of reaching out to one of your netball sponsors?'

And just like that, my networking career had begun.

Allied Pickfords, the removalist company, was one of our major sponsors, so I found the manager's number and called to ask if there were any jobs going.

'Yep, we can help you out. I'll see you Monday at 8am.'

Wow, I thought. *That was easy!*

Mum and I went straight to the nearby DFO to get me some work clothes. I got a nice top, some slacks and a pair of sensible black shoes. I felt *very* grown-up and fancy!

On Monday morning, I was dressed and ready to go by 7am and had even done my own hair and make-up (I was getting much better at this girly stuff) and drove to the Allied Pickfords offices in Dandenong. I arrived in the industrial district well before my appointment time and had a quick look around. I'd never worked in an area like this before. Actually, I'd never worked anywhere before! Sucking up all my courage, I walked into the front office.

'Hi, I'm Sharni!'

'Hey, Sharni, I'm Andrew. Welcome to Allied Pickfords.'

He gave me a quick once-over.

'You didn't bring any tracksuit pants or runners, did you?'

'Uh, no, sir.'

'Okay, well, make sure you do tomorrow. We'll go through the induction today and tomorrow you'll be out on the road with the boys.'

'Okay, thanks,' I said.

Oh shit! I thought. *What have I got myself into?*

The next morning, I was back in my familiar uniform of runners and trackies, no hair or make-up done, and at the Dandenong office at 6.30am. I quickly discovered that I was the only girl working out on the road and in the yard, and that my male co-workers were all rough as guts.

Drug testing was a weekly occurrence for some of them, and a few others had been behind bars at one point or another. A colourful and interesting workplace for an eighteen-year-old girl to say the least, but I'd long been able to hold my own around boys. Dad had taught me to stand up for myself around smart-arse males, so I had no problem giving these guys a piece of my mind when necessary.

One wolf-whistle or sleazy look and they got a spray. I used a few choice words, which I'll leave to your imagination, as I told them in no uncertain terms what they could do with that whistle. The shy, skinny beanpole girl from primary school was long gone somewhere beneath the 15 kilograms' worth of muscle I'd gained training with the Kestrels for three years. I towered over most of the guys at work, too, and my fierce female presence intimidated even the toughest of blokes – and still does!

A lovely Kiwi, George, and an old bloke named Ed soon became my mates. George and Ed were protective of me around the dickheads and joined me in telling them where to go if they annoyed me. Despite the dickheads, I never felt vulnerable. I knew these guys were just smart-arses, but then again, so was I. The work was okay, too. My job involved unpacking boxes when they came off the truck, then helping the boys unload the rest of the bigger stuff. There's a big difference between being 'weights' strong, and being able to carry couches, beds and large boxes up long driveways and umpteen flights of stairs. After only a week of this work, I had gained a whole new level of fitness.

When I was handed my first pay cheque I couldn't believe my eyes. Twelve hundred bucks after tax! *Twelve hundred bucks for a week's work*! Sure, I'd been working for twelve to thirteen hours a day, but I'd been working my bum off like that for years for free. The Kestrels had paid me $1000 a year, and now here I was getting more than that a *week*.

I instantly called my girlfriends. I was taking them out on the town this weekend!

My first couple of weeks at Allied Pickfords coincided with the last couple of weeks of the netball season. Unfortunately, things had gone from bad to worse at the Kestrels. Not only was I still not playing, but Steven Hawkins, the physio, had also booked me in for asthma tests. He'd been there when I had my very first attack on the court and was worried.

The results came in in the last week of the season. I wasn't nervous as I sat across from Steve to hear the verdict. He'd always been so kind and caring, and I trusted him.

'Sharni, you don't have asthma,' Steve said. 'In fact, there's nothing physically wrong with you at all.'

What? I wanted to scream. *How can there be nothing wrong with me? I can't frickin' breathe!* But I stayed silent. Stunned.

'It's all in your head,' Steve continued kindly.

In my *head*? So, what? I had mental problems? I couldn't make sense of what Steve was saying, but thank God the season was over and I didn't have to face my teammates again. I felt like a total idiot.

'You've been having panic attacks,' Steve explained. 'And this is obviously something we'll need to work on.'

Great, I thought, *so I'm a head case. How the fuck am I meant to fix that?*

As kind and understanding as Steve was, I decided to ignore these results and our conversation. Netball was over for the year, I was earning coin and I could go out with my friends and have fun without worrying about it affecting my training. So that's exactly what I did.

The girls and I went to a different spot nearly every night of the week. Tuesdays were at Cheers in Kew, Wednesdays were at 'The Edgy' Mentone Hotel, Thursdays were at a bar in the city (cabs were expensive from the city to Bonbeach, so I'd often shout my mates) and Fridays were at Davey's in Frankston. On Saturdays we went to The Edgy or the city, and on Sundays we'd go to the Chelsea Heights Hotel. Monday was our night off. I even ended up getting a few of my girlfriends a job at Allied Pickfords, too. Work suddenly became even more enjoyable as us girls slowly infiltrated the male-heavy workplace. Now us chicks could gang up on the guys, too!

There was something about going out to pubs and clubbing that made me feel free. For so much of the year I was never able to just let my hair down and have fun because of netball, so when I could let loose, I made the most of it! I loved dressing up for a night out and being a maniac on the dance floor. One Christmas Eve, my friend Bec and I dressed up as Christmas elves for a night at The Edgy. It wasn't a themed night. We were just feeling the Christmas spirit! Every other girl at the pub was done up to the nines, in their cute little dresses with their tonged hair, so Bec and I caused a bit of a stir when we lobbed up in our elf costumes and hit the dance floor. I couldn't have cared less about what people thought of me. I was still single but nothing I ever did on these nights out was intended to attract the attention of boys or impress them. I just loved having fun, which often involved throwing my head around and flicking my hair back and forth (I'd wake up the next morning with a very sore neck).

I always refused to touch drugs on these nights out. I *hated* them, and still do. My cousin destroyed his football career and life by using, and I didn't want to go down the same path. It's so sad that the beautiful guy I knew growing up is now someone I no longer recognise. Such a waste of life. I saw this happening and swore I'd never take drugs. I still haven't to this day. I'm not preaching, they're just not for me and, in my experience, they just do more harm than good. Okay, maybe I am preaching. Just don't do drugs, m'kay?

There have been many times in my life when I felt like the universe had my back. Even when I didn't want to listen to it or when I didn't think I was ready to hear what it was telling me. This was definitely the case when I found myself on an Allied Pickfords job during this non-stop partying period.

I always found it easy to strike up a conversation with the people whose houses I was unpacking or packing – even if I did come across photos of them holding ski equipment in the nude. The only people I found it hard to chat easily with were really cute guys.

One morning we arrived at a house for a job and I immediately regretted that I was wearing my daggy tracksuit pants, oversized polo and hi-vis vest when the guy opened his door. Damn, he was CUTE! How was I expected to unpack boxes in this dude's house all day without blushing like a … well, like a teenage girl?

I was mentally preparing myself for one of the most awkward days of my life, when he said he worked at the Victorian Institute of Sport. As I unloaded his boxes, chairs and lamps we chatted about all things sport and I soon relaxed. He was pretty chilled and easy to talk to, and I had to ignore my fantasies of us walking hand in hand along Bonbeach beach when he introduced me to his gorgeous girlfriend.

When I asked him what he did at the Institute he said, 'I'm a sports psychologist.'

No. Frickin'. Way.

I nearly dropped his expensive lamp on the spot. From that moment on I was itching to talk to him about my recent results and ask about my panic attacks. But the words just sat there at the bottom of my throat, refusing to come out. I felt too embarrassed to tell this gorgeous man that I felt like I was a bit nutty and didn't understand that what I was going through was normal. Also, I was there to unpack his house, not to fish for a free psych session, so I finished the job and said goodbye.

I was walking back to the truck when it struck me. This was my opportunity to address my issues once and for all, and I had to take it. I stopped, turned around, walked back and knocked on his front door.

'Hey, did you forget something?'

'I have mental issues,' I blurted out. 'Can you help me?'

Nothing like getting straight to the point. Well done, Sharni. Real smooth.

We stood on his brand-new doorstep and chatted for ages, and within a week or so I began seeing him professionally.

Those sessions were a total game changer for me. He helped me understand why I was having the attacks and what was causing my stress, and taught me techniques to deal with them. One of the most important things I learned was that if you don't deal with your worries and issues, they'll show up in another way. He told me a story about a psychiatrist in New York whose four-year-old daughter developed a sudden fear of the wind. They eventually discovered that she was jealous of her new baby sister but loved her mum so didn't want to show her feelings for fear of upsetting her. This particular issue manifested itself as a fear of the wind, so her psychologist encouraged her to have pillow fights with her mum as a way of releasing the anger, while having fun at the same time, and soon her fear disappeared. I could relate to this.

I was terrified of not being good enough in the netball environment and this fear was manifesting itself in these attacks. I needed to change my mindset and start thinking more positively about myself as a sportsperson. It was up to me and no-one else, but I definitely needed the help.

I started learning a lot about the power of positive self-talk and how to train my brain not to believe or listen to my negative thoughts. I realised that it wasn't just physical strength that was important in achieving what I wanted to as a professional athlete. Mental strength was and is a huge part of everything we do. A positive mindset was crucial if I was going to play netball in the World Youth Cup one day.

Times you should apologise #92

When you tell your coach that you'll miss preseason because you're going to volunteer with elephants.
(SORRY, SIMONE)

CHAPTER TEN

ELEPHANTS ARE A GIRL'S BEST FRIEND

The first step towards achieving my World Youth Cup goal was to apply for a scholarship at the Australian Institute of Sport (AIS) in Canberra. This would be an amazing opportunity, as women weren't paid enough to play sport full-time (most still aren't), and netballers in particular were only earning $1000 a year (that's $19 a week or $1.30 an hour). The AIS would be a place I could live rent-free and have all my meals provided while I got on with the business of concentrating on my netball skills. It was a very competitive scholarship. Loads of people applied every year and my chances of actually getting it were slim, but as part of my new positive mindset, I decided I had nothing to lose. I was going to go for it!

And even if I didn't get the scholarship, I knew I was ready to say goodbye to the Kestrels at the end of the year. I'd been fortunate to have three years with the team. They were an amazing group of girls who looked out for one another and who always had my back, even when I wasn't playing as well as I should have been. But I'd played a total of four games in three years, and although I was feeling better about my game and had my attacks under control, it was time to move on.

I wasn't sure what I'd do if I didn't get the scholarship, but I'd figure that out. The important thing was getting my mental health back on track. In the meantime, I'd keep training, working and saving money so I could maybe go back to uni next year.

Before I knew it, it was the end of December and I was about to head off on a trip to Thailand with a girl I hadn't seen in six months. I'd saved enough money to see me through until early February and was getting excited about the trip of a lifetime when I received a phone call.

'Sharni, you've been accepted into the AIS. Your scholarship starts in the second week of January 2007 if you accept.'

January? That's when I planned to be running around a nature park with elephants.

Shit.

I'd been looking forward to this trip for over six months and couldn't imagine not going. But I was more than a little nervous about calling my new AIS coach, Simone McKinnis.

'Hey Simone, I just wanted to let you know that I'm so sorry, but I won't be able to get to the AIS till February.'

'Oh, really, Sharni? Why is that?'

'Um ... I've got a date with a bunch of elephants.'

Luckily, Simone was very understanding and agreed to make an allowance for me.

But I didn't stop there.

'Also, I was planning on bringing my horse, Laylee, to Canberra with me. Would you be okay with that?'

There was no way I was leaving without my recently

purchased Irish Sport Horse (ISH), Laylee. It had been my dream for years to own an ISH and I finally had her.

'Um, sure,' Simone said. 'As long as it doesn't interfere with training then I have no issues.'

This coach was a boss! It was a hard phone call to make but I'd ended up coming out with everything I wanted. I'd have my long-awaited overseas trip, then return to Australia to kick off my new exciting chapter at the AIS with my baby girl, Laylee. Life was good!

The week before we left for Thailand, Maz sent me a message telling me that she and six of her friends would meet me at the airport. Thankfully these people I'd never met turned out to be awesome, which was lucky since I'd be spending a whole month with them.

When we arrived in Koh Samui, my first impression of Thailand was that it was chaotic: the traffic, the smells, the noise, the electrical wires crisscrossing over shop exteriors, the stray dogs running wild. Slightly different from the clean air and tidy streets of Bonbeach.

We checked into a backpacker's straight away. It was less than average in cleanliness and wouldn't have more than a two-star rating on Tripadvisor these days, but we were teenagers so we didn't care. The first part of the trip was all party, party, party. My new group of mates soon dubbed me 'Sharni to the EXTREME', claiming that everything I did – talk, eat, drink – was taken to the extreme.

We headed to the Viking Bar on our first night and found it was running a competition for anyone who could throw back eleven cocktail shots in eleven seconds. The winner got their name up on the board and won a T-shirt. Being the competitive individual I am, I immediately signed up, and it was an easy win. I was the Viking Bar heroine that night and the next day I wore my new T-shirt as a reminder of why I had a whopping headache.

After a few days of partying in Koh Samui, we left for the quiet and beautiful island, Koh Tao, which was a nice change of pace and atmosphere. Most of my group were into scuba diving, so while they were out on the boat I'd spend my days snorkelling and kayaking, and it was magical. We took a two-hour boat ride over to the Full Moon Party on a different island, and when we arrived at 7pm the party was going off.

There were speakers set up along the sand that pumped out loud music that changed from one section of the party to the next. We met some great people, and danced, ate and drank in the warm air. At 2am the wind changed, the temperature dropped, the rain set in and no amount of alcohol could keep us warm. We found a 7-Eleven that sold blankets and huddled together in a corner until 7am rolled around and the boat picked us up again. We were all pretty hungover by then, so the ride back wasn't quite as magical as the one on the way over. As you'd expect, there was a fair amount of spewing over the side of the boat.

Good times.

We travelled to Phuket a few days later and it ended up being a bit of a disaster. We thought it was only a four-hour boat ride from Koh Tao, so I was confused to arrive back from kayaking to find my mates yelling at me.

'YO! Pack your bags!' Maz shouted. 'We have to leave by tonight to make our flight to Phuket!'

The boat ride turned out to be twelve hours, and we first had

92

to ride into town to buy our tickets before going back to collect our bags and make it to the boat on time. Panic stations were rife! I jumped onto a manual motorbike, having no idea how to ride it and kept stalling on hills as I didn't know how to change gears. Eventually we got everything done and made it to the packed boat on time.

It was an overnight trip, so there were mattresses on top of the boat for people to crash on. Since we were so late there was limited space, and twenty of us had to squeeze under the deck with all of our luggage. There was less than a metre of space above our heads, which made for an unpleasant and *long* twelve hours.

When the boat made it to land, we discovered that we weren't even in Phuket yet, and had to endure a further five-hour bus ride to get there. When we finally arrived, every backpacker hostel was full, so we had to lug our backpacks through the streets for two hours until we finally found somewhere to stay. We were completely wrecked after our travelling ordeal, and as I was filling in the hostel form I asked Maz what the date was.

'January sixth,' she said.

My birthday. And I'd had no idea.

Worst. Birthday. Ever.

~

Maz and I bid farewell to the rest of our gang and headed off to the airport for our flight to Chiang Mai. Once again, we hadn't planned ahead, so we arrived there at 10pm with no accommodation booked. Our cab driver assured us he'd take us to his 'friend's accommodation', and as he drove through the backstreets, Maz and I glanced at each other nervously, sure we were about to be murdered. But he was an honest dude and did indeed drop us off at his friend's motel.

The next morning, we were taken to the elephant reserve at 7am and I'd never been so excited in my whole life. From the moment we arrived, the place exceeded all of my expectations. It was my dream come true. The elephants blew my mind; they were so majestic and beautiful. We stayed in treehouse huts, so they would regularly wander over to say hello, and as there were fig trees outside my room I'd feed the elephants straight from my window. Seriously, it was like a Disney movie come to life.

As volunteers we had to do work around the property, which included riding in the back of a truck to pick up bamboo rafts. When Maz and I finished loading the tray with bamboo, we realised there was no space left for us.

'How are we getting back?' We asked the driver.

'You sit on top,' he told us as if it was completely obvious.

We were slightly nervous about this dodgy arrangement, but we climbed on top of the wet, slippery rafts and held on for dear life as the truck wound its way around hairpin turns on a cliff, the edge of which was less than a metre from the tyres all the way back. When we finally got back to the reserve, I had to stop myself from kissing the dirt. I was grateful and amazed to be alive.

Everyone at the reserve got along well, and we loved our work with the elephants. We cut up their food, made massive mud baths for them to play in and then afterwards we'd play mud soccer in it with the *Mahouts* (elephant carers). We planted grass and played in the rivers with the elephants every afternoon, washing them all over with buckets and walking alongside the *Mahouts* as they took the elephants into the wild. Overnight, the elephants slept in the

Thailand bush and the next morning we had to go out and bring them all back to the property, which could take thirty minutes or three hours, depending on how far they'd ventured during the night. That time I spent with the elephants was the most magical experience of my life, and I never wanted to leave. But eventually my time was up, and it was time to head home to Australia.

When I arrived in Bonbeach, I immediately repacked my bags and headed off to the airport again, this time bound for our nation's capital and the start of my AIS adventure!

CHAPTER ELEVEN

HORSES, HOOPS AND HARD WORK

From the second I stepped foot on its paved brick entrance, I knew I was going to love living and training at the Australian Institute of Sport. I was immediately impressed by the way it was laid out; it had a huge quad that was surrounded by four-storey dormitories, with each sport having a block to itself. And everyone, from the reception staff to the athletes, was super friendly.

Yep, I thought, *I am gonna like it here!*

When I walked through the indoor netball courts, the walls were lined with photographs of my netball heroes who had trained here, and it felt like I was getting closer to my dream of playing in the World Youth Cup. Best of all, at the AIS I'd be playing netball alongside girls my age for the first time in a long time. And not only were they my age, they were also on the same journey as me as new AIS athletes. Here, I knew I'd be able to practise the techniques my sports psychologist had been teaching me without feeling too much pressure.

I moved straight into the Old Residences – a tall block of twelve rooms and four bathrooms. I can still remember the shouts of 'Shower free!' echoing down the hallways as each girl let everyone know that it was ready for the next person. There were usually anywhere between 150 and 170 athletes living in residence at one time. When teams were on tour or away, it could be as low as 30–50. Living at the AIS was great for a slob like me because I had cleaners to pick up after me – something my poor mum knew a lot about! We had a large dining hall where buffet-style breakfasts, lunches and dinners were provided for all the athletes, so I didn't have to worry about cooking for myself either. Thank God, because I'd never cooked a meal in my life and wasn't about to start. I could hang onto my juvenile lifestyle for a little while longer.

A wide range of athletes, including swimmers, soccer players, volleyballers, basketballers, boxers and gymnasts, trained at the AIS. Our sports may have been different but the thing we all had in common was our mindset. We were young, so we liked having fun, but our main focus was sport and improving ourselves as athletes. I'd heard rumours that the AIS netballers in previous years had been bitchy. I didn't know if this was true but I made a conscious decision to try and change that reputation, making an effort to introduce myself to athletes in sporting fields other than netball. Over those first few weeks, I'd head to the dining hall at mealtimes and introduce myself to whoever was there. We'd try to guess each other's sports, and most people would assume I was a swimmer or a rower because I walked around by myself. The other netballers walked around in packs and didn't really mingle with other athletes because they always had each other. A pack of netballers is quite an intimidating sight, so most people wouldn't approach them. I mean, who wouldn't be scared of a pack of strong, independent, six-foot-tall women? Most people can't handle one!

Jasmine Keene was another netballer who liked making friends with people from different sports, too. We clicked immediately and soon became inseparable. Taller than me, Jasmine had dark hair and similar features, so everyone thought we were sisters as we walked around the AIS. Jasmine would rock heels on a night out, not giving a stuff about towering over people and eventually gave me the confidence to start wearing dresses and heels, too. When I first arrived at the AIS, jeans and a T-shirt was my outfit of choice for the pub. By the time I left, my usual evening attire was a dress and heels. Thanks, Jasmine!

Our crew was made up of athletes from volleyball, swimming, basketball, water polo and athletics, and we had the time of our lives. We held 'Slip and Slide' days, where someone would get the eskies and booze, others would organise the games, and the dining hall would make barbecue packs for forty to fifty people with the works – meat, bread, salads – and we didn't have to pay a cent. Then we'd all head down to Lake Burley Griffin for the afternoon. On nights out we were allocated AIS 'house parents' who would pick us up and drop us off in the big AIS vans, and we'd usually head to 'The Arie' – the nickname for the Canberra RSL – where you could buy four drinks for $10 (bargain!). We'd stay there till ten or eleven o'clock when some would go to dance the night away at Academy – a multi-level doof-doof club – or Moose Heads, which had cheap Smirnoffs and a band in the grotty basement, where I would OWN that dance podium!

All the pubs in Canberra were on the one block, so if we went to one that was crap, we would just move on to the next. One night we all went to a place called the Uni Pub where we found a long line out the front. Our group of netballers immediately strutted to the front of the queue and announced to the security guy that we were the Territory netball team, the Canberra Darters. We were feeling pretty cocky, and were sure that we'd gain immediate entry until a dude at the front of the line yelled out, *'YOU'VE ONLY WON ONE GAME!'*

We hung our heads and did the walk of shame to the back of the line.

To be fair, we *had* only won one game, and we probably went out too much. It's no surprise there's no longer a netball program at the AIS. I don't want to take all the blame for this, mind you, as our reputation was a combined effort over the years. But yeah, I definitely contributed to the netballers' notoriety!

Other athletes were usually in training for a world cup, the Olympics or the Commonwealth Games, but netballers just didn't have that same level of serious competition because we were an underage program. The World Youth Cup we were training for was still two years away. Netballers had no major competitions to play in 2007 so the pressure was off. We were still a long way away from being in the open Australian team, which is why we partied more than those from other sports like swimming and athletics. Those guys were competing in the big leagues from a much younger age. Also, we were playing in the Australian Netball League as an Under 21s group, so it was rare for us to get a win at that point. Having said that, Laura Geitz was Captain that year, and she turned out pretty well. (Don't worry, G-Star, I promise I won't spill any stories!)

Netballers let loose on weekends because day-to-day life at

the institute could get pretty boring. We did weights and fitness at 6.30am and court work in the afternoons, and even though the training was enjoyable, it was only four hours a day. If you weren't working or studying, you'd be stuck in the concrete jungle that was the AIS a lot of the time, so days were long and repetitive.

Our strength and conditioning trainer, Gavin, worked us hard. We loved his weights programs but dreaded his conditioning sessions on the outdoor soccer pitch, especially on chilly Canberra winter mornings. Sometimes Gavin pushed us so hard that the lactic acid in my gut built up to the point where I had to duck off to the side of the pitch for a quick spew, which seemed to make Gavin very happy. It was almost as if he wasn't satisfied until one of us, usually me, had chundered. We loved him, though. He was a big softy and he cared about us.

I discovered this after I went out with a group of non-AIS friends one Saturday night. At 3am, my mate Jasmine called me.

'Sharni, where are you?!'

'Tearing up the dance floor!' I shouted into the phone. 'Why?'

'We have weights at 6am,' Jasmine said. 'You'd better get your arse home!'

I had, of course, completely forgotten about our early-morning Sunday session with Gavin. Thank God Jasmine had woken up and checked on me. I went from drunk to sober in three seconds flat and dragged myself home. I was in no state for training that morning, so my teammates covered for me when I was a no-show. But when Simone looked at the AIS swipe card spreadsheet on Monday morning and noticed that I hadn't swiped back in until 4am on Sunday and had missed training, I was caught out. She confronted me and I immediately confessed and apologised. As I did the rounds, crying and apologising to everyone in the program for my poor form, I felt deeply ashamed. I was still teary when I arrived at Gavin's office and knocked on the door.

'I heard you got on the sauce Saturday night?' he said, grinning. 'We all make mistakes, just don't do it again.'

I was so grateful for his reaction and assured him I'd learned my lesson. I wouldn't be making that mistake again.

Another new mate, Janine Ilitch, was an ex-Australian Player of the Year who I'd played with at the Melbourne Kestrels. She was also the player I'd been compared to when I was sixteen. It was so surreal to be playing with her less than twelve months after playing with her at the Kestrels. She had an amazing work ethic and attack on the ball, and I knew I wanted to be more like her. Janine kindly offered me a chance to work in the Fisheries Office making folders for her husband, Roger, so I was lucky to be able to divide my time between training, working and looking after my horse, Laylee. (I'd wondered if I might need Laylee as a happy distraction when training became a drag, and I was right.)

My days looked a little something like this:

6.30am – weights/fitness
9am – take Laylee from the stable to the horse paddock
10am–2pm – work
3pm – training back at the AIS
6pm – back to the horse paddock to muck out the stable and bring Laylee in
7pm – dinner.

Having a horse at the AIS was a novelty. And when people saw me walking around in my jodhpurs with a saddle on my arm, they assumed I was there for equestrian.

I'd take other athletes down to the stables with me to help me muck it out and they loved it. They didn't love it so much, however, when I used the communal bath to wash Laylee's rugs or when they pulled their clothes out of the dryer to find them covered in white horsehair.

Laylee kept me balanced, but looking after and riding her also burnt me out and started to affect my netball. You'd think I would have learned a thing or two from my crazy schedule the previous year, but clearly not.

She was also costing me (and my mum) a fortune. It was over $800 a month to stable and keep her, and I just wasn't earning enough to cover it. Living away from home for the first time was a huge reality check regarding money. I had held on to the horse dream for so long but now I had to make a decision. Was I going to spread myself thinly across horseriding and netball, or totally dedicate myself to the one sport I had a real chance to play on the main stage?

Laylee was a really young horse, only five years old, and eventing horses don't peak until they are between twelve and fifteen years old. When I left for Canberra, I'd been optimistic that I could both play netball and train Laylee for showjumping. My plan was to live in Canberra until the World Youth Cup in 2009 where I would represent Australia in the Under 21s team. The following year I'd be twenty-two (too old for me to get another AIS scholarship) so would move home with a seven-year-old Laylee and keep working on my goal to ride in the Olympics.

Easy, right?

Yeah, not so much.

Turns out that trying to juggle full-time netball training at the

AIS with riding and looking after my beautiful horse was much harder than I'd anticipated. I finally had to admit that I simply couldn't do both. As much as I loved horses, I wasn't in Canberra to train for equestrian, and I needed to give netball everything I had if I wanted to play at that World Youth Cup in two years' time.

Knowing this didn't make the decision – or the execution of it – any easier, though. The day I sent Laylee home was awful. It felt as if my heart was breaking and I cried all day. Sometimes the decisions that are best for us are the hardest.

When people first started coming to watch me play for the AIS Canberra Darters they'd write horrible things about me on an online netball forum. It was kind of like 'Big Footy' but for netball and we were told not to read it in case it messed with our heads. Unfortunately, I did look. I read things like:

'Sharni Layton is a crap player!'

'She'll never make it!'

'Layton is uncoordinated and unfit!'

They even gave me a nickname. 'Melman' – the giraffe character from the animated movie *Madagascar*. This was due to my awkward running style, where my knees go in and my legs swing out. Every trainer and physio I've worked with over the years has been determined to 'fix me', which really pissed me off because my scores were fine. I was among the fittest and strongest in the team, but they insisted it didn't 'look right'. As if a teenage girl isn't self-conscious enough.

My AIS trainer put it perfectly. 'Sharni, you look great standing still and you look even better when you're sprinting,' he said. 'But anything in between is just weird.'

I appreciated his honesty and that he was simply pointing out a fact without trying to change me. I tried to laugh off the horrible online comments with my family and AIS teammates, but it hurt. Luckily, I was seeing a sports psychologist in Canberra. I was fortunate that all of the extra services like psychology, nutrition, physio and medicine all came as part and parcel of the AIS scholarship, so I didn't have to worry about the costs.

Being able to see the psych more regularly helped me manage the bad feelings that came with reading these sort of comments. He was also helping me keep on top of my anxiety attacks, which were much fewer and far between once I arrived at the AIS. I can't imagine how hard it must be for budding athletes these days, with constant commentary on their performances on Twitter, Instagram and Facebook. I was playing good netball by the time social media came along, so never had to deal with that stuff as an insecure young player. There's always that part of us that wants to prove that we're good enough and that we belong, but so far, I didn't seem to be achieving either of those goals.

In September, my time at the AIS was up for the year. I headed to Melbourne and went back to working for Allied Pickfords. The plan was to earn money and do my own training during the 'downtime' between seasons. Unless you are playing internationally, there are no competitions or teams to train with during this period, so it takes a fair bit of preseason work to get back up to scratch and be ready when the next season kicks off.

I was determined to be ready to blow everyone on that netball court away.

Times you should apologise #43

When you miss training because the Charcoal Chicken line at 4am was so long ...

(SORRY, SIMONE)

CHAPTER TWELVE

DEJA VU

The chance to show off my newly learned AIS skills came at the end of 2007. A new team, the Melbourne Vixens, was being put together as part of the launch of a new Trans-Tasman competition, the ANZ Championship. This was a big deal in Netball Land, and it was hugely competitive so I didn't think I had a chance of getting in. Still, I was determined to give it a go. After my time at the AIS, I was in a good headspace and wanted to give myself the chance to be part of this new 'super team', which merged the best players from the Melbourne Phoenix and the Melbourne Kestrels.

The competition the Melbourne Kestrels had previously played in was called the 'Commonwealth Bank Trophy', made up of eight Australian teams. Liz Ellis spearheaded a group of players, who all worked together alongside the worker's union, which resulted in the first Players' Association, looked after by Bill Shorten and John-Paul Blandthorn (JP). JP became involved after attending a Kestrels training session and seeing sixteen-year-old Mel Kitchin in a moon boot with a stress fracture that was caused by overtraining. He soon learned that there were other issues, too. Australian netball players had to take time off work without pay to play games, and most retired in their mid-to-late twenties because it was too difficult to balance sport and work. JP recognised that something had to change and that the players needed all the support they could get.

The newly formed Australian Netball Players' Association (ANPA) worked together with Netball Australia and Netball New Zealand to create the ANZ Championship, replacing both the Australian and New Zealand leagues. The best part was that netballers were now paid a minimum of $10,000 a year, instead of $1000, which was a huge win for us all. This also meant that instead of eight Australian teams, there would now be just five, which is why the Kestrels and Phoenix merged to form the Vixens. As a result, the sixteen players from each team had to trial for the Vixens. Add in the three Victorians from the AIS – Melanie Kitchin, Kasey Stanaway and myself – and there were thirty-five girls in total trialling for twelve spots. You can see why I wasn't super confident about making the team.

My initial plan was to head back to the AIS in 2008, having received an offer to go back the following year. There was no limit to how long you could stay in Canberra. If you were good enough, and in the Under 21s age group, you were eligible for a scholarship every year.

I had loved being in Canberra. For the first time in years I had loved playing netball again and had made lots of great friends. So, there were mixed emotions when I received the call saying I'd made the Vixens team. Apart from being shocked and flattered, I was also a little sad at the idea of not returning to the AIS. It felt as if the netball life there had suited me much better than the one in Melbourne had, and I was happier in Canberra than I'd been in a long time.

But I also knew it would be totally mad to pass up the opportunity to join this new merged super team. It would be my first professional netballer gig and bring me another step closer to the World Youth Cup. So, I accepted the offer and prepared to move back into my family home in Bonbeach.

It was nice to be back with my family again, especially since this meant I could put off learning to cook for a little while longer. (Thanks, Mum!)

This $10,000 was a massive step up from my year in Canberra when I hadn't been paid to train, but it still wasn't enough to live on for a year. I needed to find another job. I knew from experience that working as a removalist would be too hard on my body as I started training with a new team, so what was a twenty-year-old with no other work experience to do?

Fortunately, my networking skills were still on point.

I've been a diehard Collingwood supporter my whole life and had posters of Nathan Buckley and Chris Tarrant plastered all over my bedroom wall as a teenager, so when I learned that the Collingwood Football Club was a partner of the Melbourne Vixens, I put out a few feelers. Soon, I was offered a full-time office job in the membership department of Collingwood. This was exciting not just because I would be working at my beloved footy club, but also because it was an office job and there'd be no heavy lifting involved.

Another perk was the location. The Collingwood Football Club and the Victorian Institute of Sport had obtained the Glasshouse on Olympic Boulevard for their training facilities, which included a full gym and pool facilities shared by all of the athletes.

I could arrive at work early, do my gym session, shower, change and stroll next door to start work. Sweet as!

Between working full-time and training with the Vixens I didn't have much of a social life. I had to be at work by 8.30am and it took an hour and a half to get to the Glasshouse from Bonbeach every day. Mornings were early and nights were late. When you are part of an elite sporting team, the players and coaches become your family because you don't really see anyone else. And now that I was a paid 'semi-professional' athlete, there were higher expectations on how much time I would reserve for netball. Training sessions had always been outside work hours when I was playing with the Kestrels, but now the club could push the boundaries and make our start time 4pm instead of 6pm.

As there were just twelve spots in the Vixens, I was obligated to travel with the team every week for interstate and international (New Zealand) games, even if I wasn't playing. I kept in touch with my friends through constant messaging, but I missed them all a lot. *Don't worry,* I told myself, *this time it will be worth it!*

I was twenty and it seemed as if all my years of hard work and experience were finally paying off, but secretly I was terrified and feeling out of my depth. The new Melbourne super team was a very different environment and culture to what I'd experienced with the Kestrels. The Kestrels had a nice family vibe to it, but the Vixens was much more of a dog-eat-dog world. There were a couple of ex-Kestrels in the new team, but the older girls were all ex-Phoenix players. The Phoenix team was known for its intense mindset, which was why they'd had so much success. Because the older players had the biggest influence on the team's culture, this Phoenix attitude infiltrated the Vixens team right off the bat.

The first time I met two of the best (and scariest) players, Sharelle McMahon and Natasha Chokljat, was intimidating (to say the least). The Vixens had planned a night out in the city and I really wanted to go. I was living in Bonbeach and didn't want to have to travel all the way home late at night on my own, so sent a message around to the whole team asking if I could stay at someone's house. Natasha wrote back straight away and offered for me to come and stay with her for the night. She said Sharelle was staying over, too. I was horrified.

My God! Was she for *real*?! Out of all the girls to respond first!

I couldn't turn down her generous offer, so I thanked her and arranged to get ready at her house before we headed out. When I arrived, Sharelle McMahon was already there. I sat on the couch, frozen with fear, too nervous to say a single word to either of them. And as anyone who knows me will tell you, this was unheard of. In any other social situation I could easily talk the leg off a table, but being in Sharelle and Natasha's presence that night scared me into almost complete silence.

Eventually we headed out, had a few bevvies and went dancing with the rest of the team and my nerves disappeared. Soon I was back to my usual chatty self and I was relieved to discover that my older, slightly intimidating, teammates were quite lovely and normal. For the rest of the year, Natasha and Sharelle would love to stir shit with me about how quiet I'd been on that first night, which was completely out of character as they soon discovered!

We were all friendly with each other off the court, but it was every woman for herself when it came to the team. If you weren't one of the top seven players, you were ignored by the coaches. Unfortunately, I was one of those girls and wasn't getting any game time, again.

Johannah (Joh) Curran and I were known as 'the benchies' and were often left out of court drills during training sessions. The coach would put the starting seven players on court and run through long drills with them, while the rest of us were left to our own devices on a different court. As if we weren't frustrated enough to not be playing, we now had to do extra fitness and shuttle sprints while the other girls did long court drills and practised their game plan. It seemed unfair to me that all twelve players weren't included in the team drills. It was like the Kestrels again, but worse. At least I'd felt included in the team when I was there, and had been improving my skills and fitness. Doing extra fitness instead of court work with the Vixens weren't cutting it. I was at a point where I'd been doing strength and conditioning, but without extra skills and less playing opportunities I was becoming a worse player.

Here I was again, chosen for a top team, but still not getting the opportunity to step a single foot on the court. I couldn't believe it. I knew I wasn't as good as the girls around me, but I couldn't help wondering if this was because I wasn't given any court time, which would improve my skills. I had no chance of trying to catch up.

It didn't feel as though our coach was about individual development. She seemed to focus purely on the seven players she planned to have on court in the upcoming games. If there'd been an injury, she would have been completely stuffed, but she didn't seem concerned about that possibility. In the Vixens, if you were the best, you were put on the court. Obviously, this is how most sport teams work and it's fair enough, but if I was coaching and my team was up by eighteen goals, I'd take the opportunity to put one of my 'benchies' on. This would not only keep the players' morale up, but would also show them how much I appreciated their hard work at training.

These thoughts would churn through my mind, week after week, but I never dared say anything. As the least experienced player, I didn't have the confidence to speak to the coaches, even if I disagreed with their methods or wanted to give them feedback on their coaching style. I was the new girl, so what would I know? This was how I felt anyway. It's different in every team, of course, but the Vixens coach at that time wasn't someone I felt I could approach about any of this.

If you weren't playing games at the start of the season, there was a good chance you'd never get on court, which is exactly what ended up happening to me. Joh got a bit more game time than me, but this wasn't difficult since I didn't play a single minute of a single game for the entire season. In fact, I was one of only six players in the whole league to not play at all.

Amazing stat, huh?

When we went away for games, Joh and I would muck around a bit before or after training sessions to keep life interesting. On one trip to New Zealand, we pulled an all-nighter, racing trolleys up and down the hallways of our hotel and moving heavy pot plants in front of our teammates' and coaches' doors. We thought this was hilarious until the next morning when we had to be at the airport at 4am. Not to mention getting in a heap of trouble for our pot-plant pranks.

Off the court, my teammates were great fun and we all got along really well. Our coach was Julie Hoornweg, and the girls called her Hornbag behind her back. I've never been the kind of person who talks behind people's backs, so it hadn't occurred to me that Julie might not know this was her nickname. Imagine her surprise when I rocked up for one of my first training sessions and shouted out a hearty, 'G'day, Hornbag!'

I continued calling her Hornbag for the rest of the year, completely clueless. It wasn't until No Undie Monday (the netballers' version of the 'Mad Monday' end-of-season celebrations) when the girls finally told me that I was the only one who ever called Julie that to her face.

I sat at the bar in my costume – a dressing gown to keep me warm as I'd been cold on the bench all year – eyes wide with horror as the hysterical girls explained my embarrassing faux pas. The penny dropped as to why I might have been on the bench all year. I wanted to be mad at my teammates, but it was hard since I would have been the first to laugh if the shoe was on the other foot.

I was jack of the whole Vixens thing by the end of the season. Sitting on the bench all year wasn't doing wonders for my confidence and I felt like I was wasting my life and my time. The difference this time around (in comparison to the Kestrels period) was that I had been doing work with sports psychologists for two years by this stage and I was learning how to manage my anxieties.

On the following pages are some of the key tools and lessons I learned from my psychs in these first two years.

1. **Comparing myself to me only and knowing where I was at on my own journey**
    - *Not comparing myself to Australia's best shooter (like I did when I was 16).*
    - *Have my own goals to tick off with each game. I.e. focus on keeping my shooter out of the circle or running through on the intercept. That way I could assess my game on how well I did that one skill that I was working on. This way I wouldn't beat myself up if I didn't get a rebound, as that wasn't the skill I was working on. If you improve one skill at a time, then over time you will master all of them. But if you try to improve all of your skills at once, you won't improve any of them to the standard you want.*

2. **Understanding anxiety, how it manifests and how to live and play netball without it affecting my performance or trainings**
    - *Once I knew when an anxiety attack was coming on (chest tightness) I would remind myself that there was nothing wrong with me, to breathe slowly and deeply into my belly and it would pass. By 2008, I wasn't having any issues during trainings or games because of my anxiety anymore because I knew how to tame the beast.*
    - *I trained my mind to be okay with pressure with techniques from my psychs. It didn't happen overnight, but over two years of learning how to push through, I eventually conquered it and was able to push through at games and trainings.*
    - *I realised that if I was having trouble breathing, I probably wasn't fit enough and I definitely needed to work on my fitness!*

- *Understanding anxiety was similar to how I learnt to push through physical pain when I was training with Kestrels. I learnt how to push through my mental barriers once I understood anxiety, why it was there and knowing it wasn't going to harm me and was only holding me back. That gave me the confidence to fight through it.*

3. **Taking control of my life**
   - *In 2006, I was sad because of netball, so I was therefore sad in every aspect of my life. This is allowing your mood to control your life and is a real victim mentality. So even though things weren't going my way, I did different things to pick up my mood, like having fun with Joh at training or riding my horse as an escape. I could switch off from one aspect of my life to another which made the pain of not playing more bearable. It's never healthy to have all of your eggs in one basket, i.e. if I just had netball. Because I had netball, work, family and horses, the other three baskets in my life filled me up with joy.*

4. **Surround yourself with good people.**
   - *My best friend Bec was a huge reason I got through these tough years, from the Kestrels all the way through. She didn't care that I played netball and never talked about it when I was with her. We would always go on fun adventures together and she would pay me out for my dorkiness of being an athlete. Like this time I wore runners to the three-day New Year's music festival Falls, so I could go for runs in the morning. She would joke to me like, 'Here goes the professional athlete!'*

5. **Between Bec and Katie, they both kept me grounded and made sure I enjoyed life outside of netball.**

- *My family is just a given here too. They have always supported me, no matter what choices I made, they just wanted me to be happy. Their honesty is my rock.*

Despite having these news skills and coping better and maintaining my equilibrium and mental health, my parents and friends could see how miserable netball was starting to make me (again) and were encouraging me to move back to Canberra at the end of the Melbourne season. They didn't want me to quit because they saw I still had so much potential. They also knew how happy Canberra made me the first time around, so they encouraged me to go back. I had to agree I was feeling the same way.

Aside from Bec and Katie, most of my friends were there in Canberra and I was desperately missing them, and I knew I could go back to the AIS and play as a top-age twenty-one-year-old and get back to loving the game again, like I had the year before.

One morning, toward the end of the Vixens season, I called my old coach at the AIS.

'Simone, I don't like it here in Melbourne,' I said. 'I know I won't get paid, but can I please come back to Canberra?'

Simone said she'd be happy to welcome me back, and I was ecstatic. Now all I had to do was tell Hornbag that I wouldn't be re-signing for the following season. It's a scary thing to walk into your head coach's office and say, 'Hey, thanks for offering me extra money on top of the base wage, but I think I'd rather go back to Canberra and play for free.'

It seemed like madness to give up a professional contract at this stage of my netballing career, but for some reason it made sense to me. Many people couldn't understand why I was doing it, and it didn't help that I couldn't give reasons that made sense to others. But one thing I've learnt in life is that listening to my gut instinct and my heart is more important than doing what is considered logical. In my heart of hearts, and to the depths of my gut, I knew that returning to Canberra would be best for me. I knew I needed to get another consolidating year under my belt before being fully exposed to the rigours of professional netball, and more importantly, to see if I could get back to enjoying it again. I spoke to the people who really mattered in my life - my family, friends and Simone. We went through all the pros and cons honestly together, and this process gave me faith in my own judgement to do what I knew would be best for *me* and not what might look best to people on the outside. This was my first real lesson in following my heart and I'm so glad I took the plunge.

You always hope a coach will understand your decisions, and react in the best possible way, but it didn't quite go down that way. Julie was furious and told me in no uncertain terms that I'd never be welcome in her team again.

I've never been good with bully tactics and if anything, the way the meeting went consolidated for me that leaving was definitely the best choice.

Up until this point in my career, I learned so much about the Victorian Netball Pathways. If I had known then what I knew even by the age of twenty-one, I think I would have had a different avenue into netball. Unfortunately, I believe we don't look after our young athletes well enough. There are so many that fall off the wagon due to burnout, even to this day.

I believe welfare and management of athlete loading is much better today than what it was back in the noughties, however the expectation is too high on these athletes. For example, most athletes that are training alongside a professional netball team aren't getting paid like the top ten players but are still expected to be at a lot of the sessions, and while these sessions can be labelled as 'voluntary' since the athletes aren't getting paid, if they don't go to training and other athletes do, then there is a clear disadvantage to the athlete that can't make it. Hence when I was growing up, I never would have said no to a State League training or state training session because then I might not be played over the other girls in my team, even if they weren't training as much as I was. More often than not, the other players who didn't play in multiple teams would train and play better than what I did, because they weren't exhausted from playing and training ten to fifteen days straight. It was an absolute killer.

Training isn't the only aspect that needs to be managed for younger players, but also how they are dealt with and coached. Younger athletes are at a different mental and emotional developmental stage to adults and this needs to be taken into consideration. They shouldn't be expected to ask for feedback, especially if they haven't learnt how to do this at their age. Feedback should be fed back in an educational and motivational way to help keep them on track. Of course young athletes still need to be held accountable for their training intensity and skills they are working on, but it shouldn't be expected that they just know what to do. I believe young inexperienced athletes need to be more supported than older athletes and if they're not training at the intensity they should be, it might just be because they're over-trained, which can be perceived as lazy.

Don't get me wrong; I know that all of my experiences shaped me into who I am today. But my parents put faith in the pathway to look after me (because they didn't know any different) and this was a pathway who ended up leading me (and many other athletes) to burnout at such a young age. Unfortunately, these are the athletes that don't get looked after if they fall out of the system. Kim Green has done a great job in NSW getting more support for these younger players. There has been a lot of improvement in this area with more awareness and access to wellbeing coordinators and sports psychologists, but we still have a way to go in general looking after the health and wellbeing of our young athletes.

Times you should apologise #93

When you scare the cleaners at 6am because it's easier to sleep at the office after the Christmas party rather than get an hour cab home and get back in early the next day.
(SORRY, CLEANERS)

CHAPTER THIRTEEN

TAKING A RISK

I celebrated my twenty-first birthday with a 'Sharni – past, present or future' themed party at the Collingwood Football Club. My costume was a combination of all three. In my usual style, one choice wasn't enough. I thought I still might want to be a cabinet-maker if the netball thing didn't pan out, so I sewed the top of my overalls (future) onto my netball skirt (present), with my school dress (past) underneath. I also sewed my surf-lifesaving badges onto the dress and carried a toy horse around with me all night. It was a brilliant birthday.

A bunch of friends came from interstate and stayed at our house. Because we had spent the day together, by the time we got to my party at 7pm we were well and truly in 'party mode'. I realised I'd left my iPod with all the music back in Bonbeach, as well as the piece I needed to connect to the helium machine for blowing up balloons, so my poor sister had to do the hour's drive home to get them.

But nothing could stress me out on my big night. I'd invited around seventy people and their outfits were amazing. People were dressed as senior lawn bowlers, removalists, and most of the boys wore netball dresses (seriously, boys will take any opportunity to put a dress on). Dad wasn't one for dressing up, so I'd made him a T-shirt that read, 'First there was love, then there was marriage, then there was the baby in the golden carriage … (Kara),' on the front, and '… and then there was Sharni,' on the back with a stick figure throwing up. I thought it was funny because I always seemed to be a bit of a mess.

Dad wore it with pride, and I think he appreciated my creativity more than the T-shirt itself.

My mate, Joh, dressed as a skater girl, complete with a skateboard. Before long we were sliding all over the dance floor on it, and Bec kept running behind the bar to fill super-soakers with wine and squirt everyone. It was pretty wild but I'm sure those footy club function rooms have seen worse over the years.

By the end of the night I was officially and legally a fully-fledged adult, a reality that was probably scarier for everyone else than it was for me. But I was feeling optimistic and excited about this next chapter of my life. I'd soon be heading back to Canberra to have another crack at the AIS and see my mates. Leaving the Melbourne Vixens and the ANZ Championship behind – the biggest league Australian netball and the world had ever seen – was huge, but I knew it was the right decision. I was focused, determined and ready to give netball another red-hot go! I struggle to describe where the resilience came from to keep wanting to give netball a crack. Reflecting back, it seems almost torturous that I kept on putting myself in those positions without reaping any reward. I think deep down, much deeper than many of my self-defeating thoughts; I really knew that I could make a great netballer. I just needed the right people to help me get there and I was determined to find them, to discover who I could really be. I felt I had sacrificed so much. From moving away from my friends and family, to giving up my love of horseriding. If I quit, it would have all been for nothing, or that's what I believed and felt anyway.

This determination and resilience definitely came from my dad too; it was in my DNA to never give up. Dad worked so hard at everything he achieved in life; us Laytons definitely have a fighting spirit. Another great book (yes, there are others that are as great as mine) called *Outliers* talks about how children's resilience and work ethic stems from the parents. Kara, my sister and I are 100 per cent a product of our parents' resilience and work ethic. The only difference is they fought to earn a pretty penny to give us everything we ever wanted as kids. That work ethic helped Kara own her own hairdressing salon in Malvern, Melbourne's hairdressing capital at the age of 23, and it helped me fight to become a great netballer, with every knockback making me stronger and having to believe in myself, when others didn't. This work ethis is also what gave me the confidence to walk away from Melbourne, again. I knew I needed to be playing well to make the World Youth Cup the following year, which I had been working towards. That goal was another main reason I hadn't pulled the pin on netball just yet.

In Canberra, I wouldn't be playing in a national competition like I had in Melbourne. The Canberra team had been cut when the ANZ league went from eight teams to five. Regardless, I'd be training twice a day and improving my game, which felt more important for my growth as a netballer. If I worked hard and developed my skills, maybe I'd be picked for a team I could actually play in, rather than sit on the bench every week getting splinters in my bum.

So, once again, off I went to the nation's capital.

This time I moved into the AIS New Residences. With only six girls to a block, it was a much quieter place to live. We also had a lounge room and kitchen to ourselves, a total luxury as we could now take snacks from the dining room, put them in our fridge and eat them before training.

My skills and fitness were sorely lacking, but I was determined to get them back up to scratch. I promised to be as hard on myself as my old Kestrels trainer, Stoxy, had been all those years ago. Playing with the open-aged Melbourne Kestrels and Melbourne Vixens team had severely damaged my confidence. My skills level wasn't even close to where it needed to be, and I wasn't getting the coaching I needed to improve in those teams. There had just been too many areas to work on, so it had seemed overwhelming and impossible. But now that I was playing with girls my own age, it was easy to break it down into basics and see what I needed to improve on, like footwork, reading the play and positioning my body. By focusing on what I needed to do, one step at a time, and not trying to fix everything at once, I finally started to see results.

Simone McKinnis knew what a big deal it had been for me to leave the Vixens, so from the very start she invested in me and my training. I loved Simone's training technique because it was so specific, and she focused on the things I needed to do to improve as an athlete. There isn't much time to work on the basics like footwork, change of direction or repeated efforts when you hit the big-time, so this was exactly what I needed. And Simone worked us HARD.

Our 'Welcome back to the AIS' three-day camp was full-on. We were told to pack only the bare necessities in our small backpacks, before heading off to a jungle camp at Coffs Harbour with our coaches, Simone and Sue. On arrival, we were greeted by large, angry army men who yelled instructions at us. Our bags were taken away and we were given ration packs that contained one can of beans, one muesli bar and teddy bear biscuits (random!). They told us (yelled at us) that this would be the only food we'd be given for the next twenty-four hours. We had to light a fire and take turns at keeping it alight for twenty-four hours, which meant getting up every couple of hours to make sure it was still going. If it went out, we'd be penalised the next morning.

We slept on paper-thin mattresses in two-woman tents and were given no blankets or extra clothes. It was freezing, so we ended up using each other's bodies for warmth, or going outside to sleep by the fire. (I think my tent buddy, Laura Scherian, preferred sleeping outside to being in the tent with me after I'd eaten my can of beans.) Sleeping by the fire had seemed like a good idea, until one night when Ash Brazill woke up to find a leech sucking on her face. After that, we decided it might be best to be cold in our tents, rather than be warm leech food.

On the last day of the camp, we played a game of paintball against a professional team and got annihilated. Chelsea Pitman was shot in the calf from a metre away and screamed the jungle down. I'd never seen a bruise like it then or since. It was the perfect end to what had been a shitfight of a camp.

Even Simone and Sue agreed that it was all a bit too over-the-top, and regretted taking us on it. By the time we returned to the AIS we were all ravaged with ticks, bruises and bad memories, and wanted to forget the experience as soon as possible. Unfortunately, April Brandley (nee Letton) got a reminder a week later when she found a tick in her hair.

Before we knew it, it was April and time to play our first game in the Under 21s national competition and the lead-up to World Youth Cup was on. I was played well in the first game, but in the second quarter of the second game, the unthinkable happened. As I was coming around the top of the circle to deflect the ball from my shooter's hand, my lanky giraffe-like leg got intertwined and I went flying. Instinctively I put my right hand out to stop me and I felt a huge weight go through my arm. Lying on my back, I thought, *Fuck, that hurt.* But the hurt quadrupled when I looked to my side and noticed my arm was half the length it was meant to be.

I had dislocated my elbow, which was obvious as it had popped out of the joint and my forearm (radius/ulna) had moved halfway up my humerus (which I didn't find very funny at all). All I could think was, *Fuuuuuuuuck, World Youth Cup is only four months away. Shit shit shit!*

I was in a lot of pain at this stage, but I saw Mum and Dad devastated on the sideline. I sucked it up as I didn't want to upset them, and as I walked by with the physio holding my dislocated elbow in her hand, I whispered to them, 'I'm okay, it's okay.'

But it wasn't okay. This was a huge blow that meant I could miss out on playing with the team in the upcoming Under 21s World Youth Cup – literally the only reason I was still playing netball. A dislocated elbow usually meant a six-month recovery time. I could hear the doubt in the physio's voice when he told me there was a slim chance I could make it back in time, if anyone believed I was going to make it back at all. But I did, and my coach Simone did too and that was enough for me.

The AIS environment meant that I could have daily treatment that was covered by my scholarship costs. I saw the physio every day, as well as doing my own exercises, which would have been near impossible if I was at home or in a different environment. I know now how lucky I was to receive the grade-A treatment that I did and to have so many experts looking after me.

A month after dislocating my elbow I officially made the World Youth Cup Team. That day I wrote the following in my journal:

25 May 2009
I have made the team for World Youth Cup. Finally. The reason why I never quit. The reason why I gave up horses … I am so excited. Yet I am so fucking scared. I will get my elbow right. And when I do, this is where I will write about my trip to the Cook Islands [where the World Youth Cup will be held] … WOOOOOOOOOOO!

I also stuck this quote on my wall:

'Any chance, any loss, does not make us victims. Others can shake you, surprise you, disappoint you, but they can't prevent you from acting, from taking the situation you've been presented with and moving on.
You can ALWAYS do something.
You ALWAYS have the choice – and choice can be the power.'
– Blaine Lee, The Power Principle

This sense of determination was my first step towards finding a love for netball that had never existed until then. I had no idea how powerful my mind really was and, in hindsight, that dislocated elbow was the most important and life-changing setback of my whole career.

In the months leading up to the tournament, I did bike sessions to keep myself aerobically fit. My arm was in a cast for six weeks, which was quite challenging and made it painful to run for the first week. After that, Simone and I started getting creative. I was already going to every training session, so after a month we knew I had to start stepping up my game if I was going to make it back. She would take me for extra footwork sessions away from team training to help get me back on track.

The day I got my cast off, Simone and I had a meeting with the physio. He told us that under no circumstances was I to start team training. We agreed with him, but gave each other a secret knowing look. We knew nothing was going to stop us and the following night I started training with the team again.

The team was so patient with me as I learned how to catch and throw with my left arm. I continued to train this way for the next month and was getting daily treatment on my elbow to get it back to normal. All the muscles around my elbow had seized and it was frozen at ninety degrees after having a cast on for six weeks.

I couldn't use my right arm, but I'd sometimes forget and pick up a fork to eat, getting frustrated when my hand couldn't reach my mouth! Eating a burger with two hands was out of the question. I couldn't do everyday things I had always taken for granted, like tying up my hair. The physios were working hard to try and get enough range back in my elbow so that I could at least throw and catch again.

If the girls had match-play against another team, I'd set myself up on the adjacent court and mirror the Goal Defence, mimicking every move she made for the full sixty-minute game. I looked ridiculous, playing on an empty court by myself, but I didn't care. I told myself I was going to do everything possible to recover, and I would always find an alternative way to keep up with what the team was doing. I wasn't going to give them a single reason to not take me along to the World Youth Cup in the Cook Islands.

I missed out on going to South Africa with the team for friendly matches during those three months of rehab and recovery, which wasn't great for my overall positivity. I moped around the AIS by myself for weeks but managed to get through it and maintain focus.

That first morning after my team had left, I needed to tie up my hair for a bike session at the gym but was unable to lift my arm. I strolled over to the dining hall to find one of the basketball girls, Liz Cambage, there.

'Lizzy, the netballers are gone, and I can't tie up my hair,' I said. 'Can you please help me?'

After that, Liz helped me any time I needed it while my team was away. Champ.

After three months, I defied all expectations, made it back to full fitness and played my first game of netball just one week before the World Cup. My elbow wasn't fully straight (and wouldn't be for years) but it was good enough for me to play. I was back!

As a further boost to my self-esteem, I was given the huge thrill and honour of being made Vice-Captain. I'm not sure what I was more ecstatic about: going to the Cup or the fact that I'd got myself back in time to go. I had to pinch myself as we boarded the plane to the Cook Islands. I had done it. But best of all, I had proven to myself that by goal-setting and planning, I could achieve whatever I set my mind too.

Barely anyone believed I could have made this feat, yet there I was. A big lesson from this stage of my life is that when you set goals, it's just as important to write down the processes to help you achieve them as it is to carry out the actions to get you there.

Make your goal and your processes specific and use the SMART model.

Specific	I wanted to make World Youth Cup on 8 August 2009 (pretty specific, yeah?).
Measurable	Can you measure if you achieve it? Yes, because I either would make it to the tournament or not.
Attainable	I had a dislocated elbow, so I believed it was attainable. For example, if it was an ACL injury, which requires a 12-month rehab, then this goal wouldn't have been attainable.
Realistic	I was already in the Australian U/21 team, so this was realistic (if I wasn't even in the Australian squad, then this wouldn't have been realistic because I couldn't have been selected for the team)
Time	Four months (from time of dislocation to World Cup)

Then you make a roadmap for your goal:

First month — Physio and fitness/strength everyday (guided by coaches)

Second month — Get back out on court, 2x court works a week, physio everyday

Third month — 5x court works a week, physio everyday

Fourth month — Back playing netball.

Then I could hold myself accountable.

Could I train? Yes, then great. If no, why not? What else did I need to do? Having these processes and mindset in place is tiring. Holding yourself accountable for eating the right foods every day and doing everything right to get yourself back is tiring.

But when it's only for four months and the reward is playing in the tournament you've dreamed of for years, the sacrifices and work involved to get back all of a sudden seem like a part of the reward, rather than a struggle. After I made it back and knew I was going to the World Youth Cup, my God, I was proud of myself.

Times you should apologise #28

When you eat your roommates' ice-cream and then watch them fight with each other about who ate it, and never own up that it was you.
(SORRY, GIRLS IN BLUE BLOCK)

CHAPTER FOURTEEN

THE WORLD YOUTH CUP

Rarotonga, the largest of the Cook Islands with a coastline that measures 35 kilometres the whole way around, is very beautiful. Our team was put up in a resort on the beach with the rest of the countries playing in the Cup. It was the kind of resort that had a lagoon running right through it that dropped down into an ocean where whales regularly swam. It was ridiculously perfect!

Mum and Dad came, too, as did most of our parents, which made it even more fun. We all had to constantly remind ourselves that we were there for netball, not a holiday. We weren't allowed to sunbake as it could potentially cause dehydration and affect our sporting performance, but we'd always manage to find a hidden corner in the resort for a quick tanning sesh. Sometimes we'd even hire snorkels and jump into the lagoon for a quick swim with the stunning tropical fish. It felt like more of a holiday than a netball camp, especially after our Coffs Harbour camp experience!

We had an amazing team, which included Madi Browne, Laura Scherian, Tegan Phillip (nee Caldwell), Caitlin Bassett and Amy Steele, who all went on to represent Australia. Every day we played games against countries like England, Malawi and Barbados. This would be the first of many times that I'd play against the English Goal Shooter Jo Harten. She was (and is) an amazing player and would become my archenemy in netball over the next decade. When we weren't playing games, our team would go out into the community and run netball clinics at the local schools, which was an incredible experience.

Playing in the hot and sticky climate of the Cook Islands meant having to change my dress every half. The sweat factor was real, and we'd be slipping and sliding all over the court by the end of the game. In every match, no matter how weak or strong the competition was, we had a goal to score twenty-four points per quarter and keep the opposition's score below five. There's a huge gap in the development of netball across different countries. The top countries are Australia, New Zealand, England, South Africa, Jamaica and Malawi. After the top six teams, there's a steep slide in standard, which is purely due to the lack of resources these countries have in comparison to ours.

This is why we'd train ourselves to never switch off, even if we were up by twenty or thirty goals. It was great preparation for when we came up against the harder teams. In netball, we are always taught to respect our opposition by playing our best in every single game, regardless of their skill level.

One night we had dinner with all of the Netball Australia reps. At one point, Kate Palmer, the CEO of Netball Australia, pulled me aside.

'Sharni,' she said, 'before we leave, I need you to steal me one of those giant flags.'

She pointed at a giant flag suspended on a nearby street post, about 3 metres off the ground, that read, *World Youth Cup 2009*.

Now, Kate may well have been joking, but she clearly had no idea who she was asking.

'Kate,' I said in a deadly serious tone. 'You will get your flag.'

The build-up to the Grand Final was epic. We'd won every single game in the tournament to make it to the big dance, and before we knew it, we'd reached the pointy end of the competition. I could hear the infamous words of Australian coach Norma Plummer from four years ago echoing through my head.

'Girls, the current team has just lost. You are the next age group, and YOU WILL NOT LOSE!'

Norma Plummer was at the tournament, too, and she came to see us in our hotel before we left for the Grand Final. We were all dressed in our game-day uniforms, backpacks on, shoes tied tight and hanging on her every word as she stood in front of us.

'Grand Finals are what Australia is all about,' she said. 'This will be one of the toughest games of your career to date. You need to go out STRONG and not give up! In the old Australia-versus-New Zealand fashion, it will be goal for goal, and you are NOT TO GIVE UP. You need to keep fighting until the very end, and when you least expect it to open up, it will. And YOU WILL TAKE THE GLORY!'

It was a rousing speech and it certainly did the trick. By the time Norma had finished talking, we were switched on and ready to take on New Zealand!

This is it, I thought as we travelled to the courts. *The moment I've been dreaming of for so long*. It felt like all those years of training and playing and sitting on benches had brought me here to this day. I was about to play netball in front of Mum and Dad in the World Youth Cup. That twelve-year-old girl who sat on her lounge-room floor watching the Olympics all those years ago would be so proud.

Walking out on that court was an amazing feeling. Most of the other countries had come to watch the final game, but I blocked them all out. I had a game to play and needed to concentrate. As a team, we were pumped and ready! I was confident and sure we had what it took to win. The positive energy of my teammates all around me felt so good as we lined up in front of the New Zealand team to shake hands. When the Australian national anthem played, I visualised myself not letting my player get her hands on the ball.

Not today.

We took our positions. The whistle blew. It was on!

We got stuck in, sharp from the start, and did not give an inch. When the quarter-time whistle blew, I got such a shock. It felt like the quickest fifteen minutes of netball I'd ever played. When I looked up at the scoreboard, I got an even bigger surprise. We were leading, twenty-four goals to four!

We all looked at each other. We couldn't believe it. Already it felt like all our preparation and hard work was paying off, and we went on to blow New Zealand out of the water. They came back at us throughout the game, but it was too little too late. We had our lead and we were going to take the win. When the final whistle blew, we had won by the number of goals we'd led by in that first quarter. It was unbelievable! We hugged and played stacks-on in excitement. Then I made my way over to the stands to give my excited mum and dad a big sweaty hug.

We'd won the World Youth Cup title and were bringing the

Baby me with my older sister, Kara. We look loved-up here, but the little terror on the left would grow up to chase Kara all the way home from school with long sticks, trying to whip her like a racehorse. (Sorry, mate.)

My dad, Mark, holding me here when I was just one or so. Another rebel at heart – this guy got kicked out of Year Eight for getting into a 'kerfuffle' with his teacher – Dad's always been something of a kindred spirit to me.

Mum volunteered at the Riding for the Disabled Association of Australia, and this was two-year-old me riding one of their horses, Fudge. I was smitten! Love the stackhat.

My first-ever gold medal! Four-year-old me (front left) proud as punch after a surf-lifesaving competition.

First day at Bonbeach Primary. Don't let the angelic smile fool you: I was a nightmare child prone to terrible tantrums, which would see me take out my rage on a tree in our back paddock.

Here I am (front, centre) with Sandy, my gorgeous first pony, in 1998. I loved mucking around with my pony club friends – including a few missions through the McDonald's drive-through, naturally!

My mixed 11/U Chelsea Rep team. Can you guess which one is me? Yep, the tall noodle in the middle. I really got a taste for competition with these guys.

I was always a staunch tomboy, so I suspect my older sister, Kara, was behind the spiffy makeup and hair-do in this glamour shot from when I was twelve.

I'll always be a horse girl at heart. Showjumping state selections here with my beloved horse Billy in 2002. We went on to come sixth in the state.

Never much of a girly girl, I loved getting away to Wilsons Prom every Cup weekend with my Bonbeach Beach crew (I'm second from the right). Not quite sure about the hand gestures here, but I was always laughing with this gang.

My very first Kestrels player card in 2005 with an inspiring message for my friend Katie: 'Good luck with stuff'. Our preference for boys' clothes and Blink-182 meant we were destined to be lifelong mates.

With Jasmine Keene at the Australian Institute of Sport (AIS) in 2007. Being at the AIS, where my netball heroes had trained, was a dream come true. The cherry on top: the Adelaide Thunderbirds selected both Jasmine and me.

In 2007, I made the Australian 21/U Netball Team for the first time. Talk about pinch-me moments! I was just nineteen and pretty much in awe of everyone in this photo. I'm right in the middle of the back row – seventh from the left.

This moment in Singapore in 2011 was pretty surreal: the first open World Cup I ever played in – and we won! (Credit: Dave Callow.)

Another netball career highlight: winning the 2013 Grand Final with the Adelaide Thunderbirds. (Credit for both photos: Richard Keane, Sports in Focus.)

Nothing beats moments like this! Such joy seeing all our hard work pay off with an epic gold medal (see below!) at the 2014 Commonwealth Games.
(Credit for both photos: Michael Bradley).

Game face on at the 2015 Netball World Cup tournament in Sydney!
(Credit: Netball Australia.)

The squad basking in our 2015 World Cup win in Sydney. I didn't get a gig in the
Grand Final, but I'm proud of how I performed in the semis. You learn to put aside
your ego in situations like this; it's about Australia, not just you.
(Credit: M.W, Netball Australia).

Being the lankiest player on the court has its advantages! These photos were taken at separate Constellation Cup tournaments (the netball equivalent of rugby's Bledisloe Cup): above is 2015 (credit: Dave Callow), below is 2017 (credit: Narelle Spangher).

It was an incredible honour to captain the Australian side in 2017's Quad Series, even though it made me scared shitless, to put it bluntly. I second-guessed myself the whole way, which made me feel like a weak and indecisive leader – even though the team performed brilliantly and we won the tournament. (Credit for both photos: Getty).

Courtside smooch with Luke Norder, my now-husband. This was my last netball home game in Melbourne in 2018. And, yes, Luke and I are in matching dresses: to support me on this milestone, he and his mates all wore the uniform!

With Mum, Dad and my sister, Kara, at my netball retirement announcement in 2018. They had stuck by my side through my greatest wins and my darkest lows, so it was only fitting they helped me farewell the sport I'd played for fourteen years.

This book wouldn't be mine without a photo to honour this chick, my best mate, Bec Hudson. Before I met Luke, Bec would always be my hot date at events like this, the 2017 Collingwood Magpies AFLW awards night. I wouldn't be the person I am today without this gem.

The Collingwood VFLW side's 2019 premiership, defeating the Western Bulldogs. Nothing beats this feeling, shared here with our captain, Grace Buchan. I even contemplated retiring after this moment because it was just too good.

Wrangling a Sherrin was a learning curve, but I loved getting stuck into this new sport. This was a 2020 AFLW semi-final match against North Melbourne. (Credit for both photos: Collingwood Football Club Media).

In 2020, celebrating my first-ever goal with aeroplane arms! Such an iconic moment for this netballer-turned-footballer. I'll never forget how my teammates got around me.

Marvel Stadium, 2020. People often judge my ball drop, but ya know what? I'm thirty-three and nothing's perfect, so I'm not going to try and fix it now! This lady is a far cry from the obsessive perfectionist she once was. (Credit for both photos: Collingwood Football Club Media).

I'm proud of my achievements, but nothing compares to marrying Luke Norder on 1 January 2021 (after I'd finished this book).

I can't wait for our adventures as husband and wife. We married in the 'COVID normal' era and took Dan Andrews's advice to 'get on the beers' very seriously at our wedding. (Credit for both photos: Miranda Stokkel).

trophy back to Australia, where it belonged. One by one we were handed our trophies in the after-match ceremony. I felt so proud and knew I'd hold this moment in my heart and mind forever.

Back at the resort, our parents presented us with singlets with *World Youth Champions '09* printed on them. They'd decided it was worth the risk to pre-empt our win. We were chuffed and put them on straight away for the afterparty. This is one of the best parts of any tournament. It's a chance for athletes to finally let out all that tension and worry that has been building up for so long. And when you've won, it's even better! We all had a blast that night. All of the players from each country came together to celebrate and have a boogie. There were no enemies or grudges that night. We were all friends now.

Our flight home was at 1am that night so we had a good time, but not a long time. As the cab drove us back to the resort to get our bags and head to the airport, I looked up at the *World Youth Cup 2009* flags on the street.

That's right! I thought. *I promised Kate I'd get one of those for her!*

The flags were too high up on the poles for me to be able to cut them free. A few hundred metres from our resort I spotted two flags that had fallen. The bottom half was still attached to the pole, but the top had flopped over. I could reach it!

'STOP!' I yelled.

The cab came to a screeching halt. I told my confused teammates that I'd meet them back at the resort and jumped out. The fallen flags were outside a hotel and bathed in full light, so I couldn't be as discreet as I would have liked. But I didn't have time to worry about that. I began yanking on the flag, trying to pull it free from the pole.

'Oi, what you doing?!'

Five huge guys, who I assumed were locals, were standing across the road staring at me.

'What does it look like?' I shouted back, pulling on the flags. 'I'm trying to steal these flags. Are you going to help me or not?'

I probably should have been more cautious, and less sassy, in this particular situation, but I was on top of the world that night and scared of nothing and nobody.

The guys turned out to be lovely and more than willing to help a stranger steal a flag in the dead of night.

Between the six of us, we succeeded in getting the flags off the pole. My second win for the day! But now we had another problem. The metal bars attached to the flags had come off with the flags and I couldn't very well fit those in my suitcase. One of the guys pulled out a lighter and melted the cable ties off, freeing the flags from the bars. Done!

I had kept my promise to Kate and couldn't have been happier! I knew I didn't have a lot of time before the bus left for the airport, so I thanked the guys for their help and sprinted back to the hotel.

Everyone was in the lobby, dressed in their uniforms and ready to go, when I ran in. That's when I realised that, in typical Sharni fashion, I was the only one yet to pack my bags and was still in my party clothes. Oops.

Steve, our physio, rolled his eyes at me. 'Sharni, go and get changed!' he shouted.

Still feeling on top of the world, I stripped down to my bra and undies, the flags draped around my neck, and pretended to be Superwoman.

My roommate, Sophie Croft, quickly dragged me away to our room, got me dressed and helped pack my bag.

Walking to the bus, I spied Kate Palmer.

'Hey, Kate!' I yelled. 'I got your flags!'

Judging by her expression I wasn't sure she believed me, which turned out to be a good thing as I had grown very fond of my flags by then. I decided to keep them for myself and proudly hung them on my wall when I got back to the AIS.

Times you should apologise #89

When your roommate at the World Youth Cup has to pack your luggage because you're too busy stealing flags and running around in your undies.
(SORRY, SOPHIE)

CHAPTER FIFTEEN

LEAVING THE AIS

I didn't have long to savour the high of winning the World Youth Cup, just a few weeks in fact, before my time at the AIS came to an end. I was at a crossroads; I wasn't sure what I wanted to do and didn't have many options.

After six years and three teams, I had reached a crisis point in my netball career. Did I want to continue on this path of a netballer? Or give it away to follow my dream to be an Olympic Equestrian rider? The latter was slipping further and further from my grasp the longer I wasn't riding.

I wasn't sure if I wanted to continue as a netballer, because as an athlete, you sacrifice a lot. You miss a lot of friends' birthday parties, weddings and other events, and even if you do get to go, you better stay on the soda waters all night. You can't go out on weeknights, and if you do, your coach will find out and punish you, along with the added guilt trip that you've let your team down (been there, done that).

Even after all this, there was never a guarantee that I would still 'make it' to the top level. The team is always your number one priority in team sports, which is worth it when you are seeing success, but it's a massive drag when you're not. And I had achieved my dream that I had been striving for, for the last four years. It was time to revaluate what was important to me, and what I wanted to strive for over the next four years of my life.

I had to decide if I wanted to keep making these sacrifices for a sport that I felt I wasn't that into anymore. Although winning the World Youth Cup made me realise that the hard yards *are* worth it. The enjoyment I felt from winning that tournament for Australia, especially when the group four years prior hadn't been able to achieve the same feat, was nothing like I had ever felt before. I had the taste of success and I had a niggling feeling that I wasn't ready to give up on netball just yet.

But then there was a huge part of me that just wanted to be with my family, friends and horses, and live like a normal person again, without the judgement and endless sacrifices. I was torn because when I played netball, I missed the family and connection that came with being a 'normal' human that didn't have to live away from home and I didn't know if I could keep doing what I had been over the last six years.

When I was at netball I wasn't as happy as I was when I was just living life as a normal human. So you can imagine the conflict I felt inside. Do I do what makes me happy, or do I continue to sacrifice the things I love to see how great I can really be?

I'm unsure why, but I'm glad I had the foresight to realise that although I might not be as happy now grinding away and working towards my dreams, I had a feeling that I would be in more pain and even unhappier if I got older and realised that I'd given up on reaching my full potential. What would seven-year-old year old

Sharni say if she saw I had the opportunity to be a professional Australian athlete and I gave it up because it was all too hard? I bet she would be pissed. Mind you, seven-year-old Sharni also thought it was probably going to be an easy ride to the top.

I was almost twenty-two, and I was closer to being able to achieve this dream of representing Australia through netball than horseriding. Equestrian was a dream that seemed to continually be slipping further from my grasp. And that determined mind inside me was telling me that I couldn't quit netball without knowing what I could truly achieve. My need and drive for sporting success was stronger than the desire to be back to normal with my friends and family and that was what made me realise I needed to give netball just *one last chance*.

I wasn't the only one left chasing my dreams with my future up in the air. There were twelve of us from the AIS were in the same boat. We were all worried about what lay ahead for us and whether or not we would have careers as professional athletes. We were playing in the Australian Netball League – a national development league underneath the ANZ Championship – and the stresses of whether we were going to be picked up in a professional side started eating its way through the team with bitchiness and jealousy. Some were getting offered contacts and others weren't. It was an extremely scary time for all. Had we reached the peak of our careers? We didn't know.

Some girls were honest with us about the conversations they were having with coaches, and others were keeping things to themselves. My good friend Amy Steele was a better defender than me, and we had talked openly and decided we wanted to go to different clubs. If we went to the same club, it was unlikely we'd both have a chance to play, and there was way more chance that the person on the bench would be me. I am still grateful now to Amy for being so honest and sharing her thoughts with me around her decision-making process. Thanks to our open conversations, and our mutual love and respect for one another, I was aware of where Amy wanted to go, which meant I could work out what was going to be best for me.

Amy was hot property and had every team chasing her: Brisbane, Melbourne, Adelaide and Perth. I had three teams, Melbourne, Adelaide and Perth, chasing me. Despite my coach's vow to never have me back, I was offered a spot with the Vixens again, but I didn't want to go back to an environment that hadn't served my life and career thus far.

The next phone call I received was from Jane Searle, my old Kestrels coach, who now coached West Coast Fever.

'Sharni, we'd love to have you, but we want Amy more,' she said. 'So, if she decides to go elsewhere, we'll take you.'

This was becoming a familiar refrain and starting to mess with my self-esteem. I didn't hold it against Amy – it wasn't her fault. Plus, she couldn't play with every team, so I was in the fortunate position of being a backup. Still, the knowledge that I was always the second pick was pretty shitty, especially after how hard I'd worked to get to where I was.

Then the next phone call came in.

'Sharni, it's Jane Woodlands-Thompson from the Adelaide Thunderbirds.'

I braced myself.

'And I would love to have you as part of my team,' Jane continued.

'Um, what? But what about Amy?'

The words were out of my mouth before I could stop them.

'Amy is great,' Jane said, 'and we'd love to have her, too. We could just have you, or both of you, but we definitely want you.'

Phew. Someone saw me for me. Jane recognised the work I'd put in, the player I was and the player I knew I was going to become.

I was seen.

A few minutes later I got a call from Jasmine.

'Sharni!' she yelled. 'I just got offered a contract with the Adelaide Thunderbirds!'

That sealed the deal.

We squealed like twelve-year-old girls. The Thunderbirds wanted me, AND my best friend was coming, too. As far as I was concerned that was as good as it was going to get.

I still felt a pull towards Melbourne, though, because my family was there, so I went to my AIS coach to get her advice.

'Simone, how do I know if I've made the right decision?'

'Make a decision, but only tell your nearest and dearest,' she said. 'Then sleep on it and you'll know the next morning if you made the right one or not.'

That night, I talked to Mum.

'Mum, I've been thinking about it and I'm feeling like I might move back to Melbourne.'

She was ecstatic, but as soon as the words were out of my mouth, it felt wrong. I actually felt sick to my stomach, but as Simone had suggested, I slept on it. When I woke the next morning, I knew in my heart that I couldn't move back to Melbourne.

Mum was making a cup of tea when I walked into the kitchen.

'Mum, I'm moving to Adelaide.'

Mum's face dropped. She had got her hopes up that I was moving back home. Even though she was disappointed, she also knew I was making the right decision for me.

That day, I called Jane Woodlands-Thompson to accept the Adelaide Thunderbirds contract.

CHAPTER SIXTEEN

ADELAIDE, PART ONE: UNASHAMEDLY SHARNI

I didn't know what to expect when I moved to Adelaide. The only times I'd ever visited were for netball tournaments when my teammates and I drove around in the team bus counting all the churches. So many churches!

I have nothing against religion, but my Sunday mornings are for sleeping in, so I was interested to see what else the City of Churches had to offer. I'd heard Adelaide described as having a 'country-town feel', but I'd been living in Canberra so any town would have to be an upgrade.

Okay, calm down, Canberrans. I LOVE Canberra. I know you have Lake Burley Griffin and a tonne of roundabouts, but I'd soon discover they didn't quite compare to Adelaide's beautiful beaches and wineries.

The first thing I noticed about Adelaide was its charm and relaxed vibe, and I knew this place would suit me just fine. I'd never enjoyed the hustle and bustle of big cities like Melbourne or Sydney, and Adelaide's calm atmosphere felt like the perfect place to have one last decent crack at my netball career.

The best part about moving to Adelaide was being there with my best friend, Jasmine Keene. We moved into a small house on the beach near Glenelg, as we were both beach bums at heart. The Thunderbirds supplied us with beds, and we were rapt. Now, this may not sound very exciting, but when you're twenty-two years old and have your first queen-sized bed in your first 'adult' house (not a dormitory like at the AIS), it's a big deal. When I walked into my room and saw the bed, I leapt up onto it and started jumping up and down, as anyone 'adulting' for the first time does …

But apart from the beds and a couple of beanbags, our house was furniture-free. Before leaving Canberra, I'd bought some stuff from a friend but that was a few weeks away from arriving. So, on our first night, Jas and I decided to go and explore our new city, rather than sit on our beanbags and stare at the wall all night. We were on a mission to make some new mates, having left all our old ones back in Canberra, so we slapped on some make-up and headed to the Jetty Bar on the Glenelg strip.

Standing at the bar with our drinks, we scanned the room for potential candidates.

'Nope, they look too bitchy.'

'Nope, they look too drunk.'

'Nope, they look too annoying.'

We were pretty damn judgey and picky for two six-foot-plus girls who were new in town.

We spotted three nice-looking young blokes sitting at a table who seemed to be having an interesting conversation, so we wandered over to get involved.

I shot them my friendliest grin. 'The water here in Adelaide is a bit shit, don't you think?'

I was silently congratulating myself on this awesome conversation starter when I noticed their confused expressions. Hmmm, maybe not the best opening line.

Then one of the guys grinned back. 'So, I assume you two aren't from here?'

Phew.

'No, but we've just moved here and don't know anyone.'

'Wanna join us?'

And just like that, Jas and I found ourselves some new mates for the night. But what we didn't know then was that Dan and Pethick would turn out to be lifelong mates.

After the Jetty Bar, we all kicked on to 'The Grand' – a hotspot in Adelaide at the time – where we were introduced to even more people and boogied all night. I wasn't drinking so I offered three of the guys a lift home at the end of the night. By the time we got to the last house, Dan's, Jas and I had noticed something all the houses in Adelaide seemed to have in common.

'Hey, Dan, why are Adelaide houses so old-looking?'

'Hey,' he said defensively, 'the sandstone may make them look old, but they're schmicko inside. Wanna come in and have a look?'

So, Jas and I headed into our new friend's house at 1am on a Saturday morning only to find his parents sitting in the kitchen.

'Sharni, Jas,' Dan said, 'this is Shaz and Tony.'

The front door opened behind us and Dan's sister, Nikki, walked in. Next thing, the kettle was on and the six of us were getting to know each other over cups of tea in the lounge room.

'What do you mean you have no furniture?' Shaz said, horrified. 'Do you want to borrow one of our TVs and a DVD player?'

I was mortified. 'It's 1am and I'm a total stranger, Shaz. I can't take your stuff!'

Then, after a pause.

'But I could come back tomorrow and grab them then if that's okay?'

The next morning, Jas and I drove back to their house to pick up our new goodies. Once we'd loaded the car, Dan and his mate Matt insisted on taking us on a driving tour of the Adelaide beaches. When we dropped Dan off later that day, Shaz ran down the driveway, a covered dish in her hands.

'Girls! I'm sorry I'm heading out, but I cooked this spinach pie for your dinner!'

We were overwhelmed by the Lunniss family's kindness and couldn't believe our luck. How had we managed to meet the most generous people in Adelaide (possibly the world) on our first night out in a new city?

Over the next few years I spent many nights with the Lunniss family. To this day, I consider Tony and Shaz my Adelaide parents, and Dan and Nikki my Adelaide siblings. It feels as if I've known them forever, and I'm so lucky to still have them in my life. Sometimes having a loud mouth and an inappropriate opening line pays off!

But, as fun as it was, I wasn't in Adelaide to go out and meet awesome people every night. I was there for one last-ditch effort at kickstarting my professional netball career. So, after that first weekend in Adelaide, I got my priorities sorted and the hard work began.

I was back to a minimum-wage contract of $10,000 a year, so I took a job as a receptionist and salesperson at a solar company with one of our sponsors to help boost my income. Playing with the Thunderbirds also meant I wouldn't be able to play in my preferred position, Goal Keeper, as two of the best defenders in the world, Mo'onia Gerrard and Geva Mentor, happened to be in my team.

I'd have my work cut out for me trying to compete with them. Still, I was determined to do everything I could to improve my game to benefit the team, as well as myself. After my double-stint at the AIS, I'd come to Adelaide with one mission in mind:

This will be my last crack at trying to play netball at the professional level. If I don't end up playing on the court and end up sitting on the bench again for another year, then I'll quit and finally go back home and continue riding horses.

Once again, the universe was on my side. Jenny Williams, the owner of the Adelaide house Jas and I were living in, was a sporting champion herself. She had played and coached for Australian teams in Lacrosse, as well as multiple other sports for her native South Australia. As such, she is in the South Australian Sports Hall of Fame. More than that, Jenny is a sensational sports psychologist and all-round great bloody human. I had scored myself not only a good sports psych, but the best in the business, as well as a new great friend.

I had continued seeing the AIS sports psychologist once I moved back to Canberra, but having moved so many times, I was becoming frustrated having to leave them. On the following page is what I learned about myself in my middle years of sports psychology.

1. **How to stay in the moment during a game**
   - I used to beat myself up mentally if I made a mistake in a game. But I learnt that dwelling on mistakes only creates more mistakes. For example, if I threw a ball out of court, I'd get angry. And when the person who took the throw in, passed it straight to my shooter under the post and she got a goal it made me feel even worse. Then I realised that if I threw the ball out of court, I could clap my hands together, which was a technique to force me to let the mistake go and get my concentration back on my player. That way, I could potentially get the intercept before the other team scored. Winning.
   - Another technique I used was to have a hair tie or elastic band around my wrist during training. If I stuffed up a drill or threw a ball away, I'd flick the band against my skin and the sting would bring me back to the physical, out of the mental, and get my head back in the game.

2. **Keep pushing myself, even when I'm tired**
   - I used to give up in fitness or drills when I couldn't keep up. So, I changed my mindset by thinking to myself, 'I bet you can't do another sprint!' and challenge myself to do it. I turned the pain of pushing myself into a game. This made it more fun and was more rewarding when I achieved that extra rep on the court or in the gym. This is where my 'never give up' attitude on the court really came into its own, and I ended up becoming known for it being a trademark of my game.

3. **How to stay relaxed between games**

- Did you know, if you think about a game/interview/ stressful situation in your mind, your body plays it out energetically? So, if you've ever had one of those games where you've rocked up feeling exhausted, as though you've already played a game, chances are you've played it in your head. Whenever I felt tired and drained before the game had even started, it affected my performance. So, I learned to write down what I had to do for a game (stay in front of my player, push her to the side) without playing the game over and over in my head. You may be able to relate to this to other aspects of your life, like an interview or public speaking. Then I had to find something that would relax me the night before, like listening to calm music, watching a show I liked or chatting to family and friends. It's all about learning what works for you.

As a result of all the hard work I'd put into my netball mentally and physically, I was rewarded at the start of January 2010 by being invited to the Open Australian Team training camp. I had made another step forwards and couldn't believe it when I received a call from Norma Plummer, the head coach, to invite me along to the camp.

The whole experience was crazy and intense, and a good eye-opener in terms of how far I still had to go if I wanted to play for the Open Australian Team one day. The training sessions were longer and more intense. There was a lot more video analysis of other countries' teams playing than I had ever been exposed to before. There was also a greater focus on being an elite athlete and we were expected to get better results in fitness testing (boy, did I have way to go in this department) and we also had to get our skinfolds done. Skinfolds are something every athlete must do and most hate – both males and females. A dietician uses callipers to measure how much fat you have over seven sites of your body – your pecs, subscapulars, triceps, abdomen, hips, quadriceps and calves. They then add these numbers up and basically tell you how overweight you are.

In a nutshell, it sucks.

The skinfolds of girls in the Australian netball team were under 80mm, but mine was over 100mm. I felt like the dietician was highlighting that I probably needed to be fitter if I wanted to make the Australian Team, which was absolutely true. But as an obsessive-compulsive 22-year-old, I interpreted that as me needing to lose weight if I had any chance of making it professionally.

It was true I'd spent the last few years consuming alcohol and junk food, and I'd definitely put on weight, especially after dislocating my elbow, but seeing the actual number was a shock. I'd never been told I was overweight in my life, but since I'd promised myself I'd give netball everything this year, I gave myself no choice but to get that number down.

Being the driven person I am, I instantly gave up drinking and eating bad food, and this was the beginning of an obsession with losing weight that would eventually lead me down a toxic path.

I got back to Adelaide and began my new 'healthy' lifestyle by basically starving myself. I was eating, but definitely not carbs or anything that had *any* sugar in it and my portions were very minimal. My 'treat' was one coffee, with milk, a day. The lack of food didn't seem to affect my training though. I slotted straight in with the Adelaide Thunderbirds. The girls were fun and I was really enjoying training. It was like nothing I had done before and every session was different and interesting. I was definitely enjoying my netball more than I ever had. I even got to the stage where I didn't mind if I didn't get to play because I was enjoying it so much.

By the time the first game rolled around, as expected I was on the bench, but as I said, I felt okay about it for some reason. We were playing well, but then before the end of the game, the Wing Defence went down, having done her Achilles tendon. It's horrible to say that one woman's misfortune is an opportunity for another, but I decided to grab my chance. Wing Defence was a position I'd never played before, but the following week I went straight to the coach and told her I was willing to give it a shot. If there was anything that I had learned from my Kestrels and Vixens experience, it was that if I wanted an opportunity, I needed to speak up, no matter how scary and daunting it may be. No-one else was going to do it for me.

'Jane, I know I don't play Wing Defence,' I said, 'but I'd love to learn. Is there an opportunity there for me?'

Jane told me to come in and do some extra training sessions that week and we'd see how it went. It wasn't a yes, but it definitely wasn't a no, and I vowed to own that WD bib!

From then on, I did all the compulsory training sessions, as well as extra sessions in the gym and one to two extra sessions with Jane every week. Not only did I want to learn this new position to the best of my ability, but I also wanted to be better than the girl who had played it before me. Wing Attacks are the fastest players on court, so I needed to up my footwork skills to keep up with them, especially considering my height. Wing Defences weren't known for being the tallest girls on the court. I did a lot of short quick-feet and change-of-direction drills in training, using ladders and cones. I also had to do a lot of work around landing on the circle edge without going offside, as I was so used to running straight into the goal circle as a Goal Keeper.

Aside from having the opportunity to train and play under my coach, Jane Woodlands-Thompson, another bonus of moving to Adelaide was training with Lisa Alexander. Lisa was assistant coach of the Thunderbirds team but had also been my coach in the Under 21s Australian program. She knew me well, affectionately called me her baby giraffe, and pushed me hard. Having coaches like Jane and Lisa, who believed in me, was a big part of my mental shift that year and why my confidence started to improve.

I'd love to say that believing in yourself is enough, but that wasn't the case for me. Confidence comes from experiences, and when they have been more negative than positive, it's hard to back yourself. If you're lucky enough to have a network of people around you who truly support and believe in you, like I did in Adelaide that first year, this is what solidifies your self-belief. Jane and Lisa knew what I needed to learn to become a great netball player, and their confidence in me dampened the negative thoughts I had about myself. Just a month after joining the Thunderbirds, I was given one of the five leadership roles in the team under our Captain, Nat von Bertouch, and this was a huge confidence boost.

I was wearing the WD bib when Jane put me on for my first-ever professional game with the Thunderbirds. I was nervous, but also felt ready after all the extra training I'd been doing. As the game got underway, it seemed that all my hard work was paying off, but I soon realised that playing at this level was a step up from what I'd been used to. I just didn't have the fitness to run out a full game, so was subbed off at half-time.

I'd played well, though, and seeing how happy Jane was with my performance was the best feeling in the world. We won that game and there was a lot of hype around the fact that I'd played Wing Defence. The Wing Attack had found it difficult to feed the ball into the circle because she couldn't see the shooters over me. I'd also gotten a lot of tips and touches so there was a lot of positive post-match talk about the 'tallest Wing Defence in town'. It felt so good to hear these positive comments about my game.

After that first match, the coaches put a program together to keep me physically fit, as well as to improve on my jump. Even though I was playing Wing Defence, my ultimate goal was to be back in Goal Keeper, so I wanted to improve my vertical jump to combat the giant Jamaicans we'd be playing against.

When the six-foot-four-plus Jamaicans first entered our league in 2008 it was a big wake-up call for the Australians. Before this there had only been one tall shooter in Australia, Caitlin Bassett, who was my age and still considered a baby in the netball world. It was a bit of a shock to everyone when these amazingly skilled, tall Jamaicans began dominating our league, as no-one had figured out how to properly defend them yet.

It soon became clear that it was going to be a group effort to stop these tall shooters. The Thunderbirds had to get technical! To try and stop the ball landing perfectly with the shooter, everyone in the team had to push the Jamaican players high and wide to keep them as far away from the circle edge as possible. This tactic would force the centre-court players to throw the ball from further away, which would give our Goal Keeper a greater opportunity to come around and intercept.

I wanted to be one of the first, if not *the* first, defender to learn how to jump as high as the tallest girls in our league and take them on, mano a mano! I wanted to make a difference in both the competition and netball in general.

Unlike my time at the Vixens, I was being put on court to play games, which was boosting my confidence and developing my skills. Once I had my personal goal to jump as high as the Jamaicans, I refused to listen to anyone who told me I couldn't do it. If anything, I took the words 'you can't' as a challenge.

Netballers weren't renowned for being able to jump high, but after being around volleyballers at the AIS I'd learned a lot. Volleyballers had to train to get that kind of jump, since it doesn't come naturally. That is, unless your name is Kate Shimmin. Kate has the most ridiculously high natural vertical jump I've ever seen and is known as the 'Rejection Queen'. If Kate and the volleyballers could do it, why couldn't I?

I went to see someone who specialised in this area and soon discovered that it was my technique, not my strength, holding me back. We made a plan to change the way I was training by learning the right techniques. For example, I had to change the way I did squats. Instead of just adding extra weights to the squat bar and squatting 100 kilograms, I had to learn how to use my muscles properly. I had to make sure my knees didn't bend in, focus on getting my bum lower and stretch properly before I jumped. That way I would get full use of my muscles, and the best out of my body. It was a huge lesson for me. If I wanted to get better, I had to slow down and focus more carefully on my jumping technique. Being the fast and lanky giraffe that I was, and had always been, with my limbs flailing all over the place, this was a new way of approaching my game.

I also made an effort to seek out footage of a defender who had played well against an upcoming Jamaican opponent. I'd watch what they had done in the game, notice what techniques and gameplays had worked best, and then adjust my training around that. It was also a good way of studying my opponent before a game to find out what she liked doing and how she played. This meant I could do my best to stop her from using those skills and tricks when I was on her. My coach taught me to write down two to three key points for each player I would be coming up against that week, and keep it in my backpack to take to practice matches. As the teams were called out, I'd listen to the name of the girl I'd be playing against and then take a quick look at my notes. It might say something like, 'Madi Brown – loves the left side of the court and catching the ball deep in the goal third.' Then I'd know going out that I'd need to push her to the right and keep her in front of me so she couldn't get that high ball over me, or force her there so I could catch a high ball over the top of her because I was taller.

Our team did our training at a gym called 'FastTwitch' with two trainers, Damo and Andy. We did all our strength and power training there, and I was so grateful for all the time Damo and Andy invested in me. The gym had machines that activated the fast-twitch fibres in your muscles. After building muscle through a standard gym program, you'd then use these machines to activate and build the number of fast-twitch fibres. The machine would help you learn to run faster, and it would measure your improvements. I couldn't believe the strength and power I started to feel after a few weeks of training this way at the gym. It was an incredible feeling and I loved it.

Damo and Andy also helped me work on my jumping technique. They quickly discovered that my biomechanics – how I ran and jumped – were appalling. This was no surprise to me! They started me on a program to strengthen my glutes (our power machines) so I was doing heaps of squats, deadlifts and power cleans. As for improving my running technique, they would make me stand next to a wall for twenty minutes at a time, lifting my leg up and down in front of a mirror to make sure my knee and foot were straight. It was much harder than it sounds and taught me a lot about patience! I did these exercises five days a week until running began to feel more natural to me, then I had to keep doing them to make sure I didn't lose the technique I'd learned. What they say is true: if you don't use it, you lose it!

They taught me how to use my arms to get to the highest point of the jump to reach the ball. I used a ball for all of my jumping sessions because, for some reason, I could always go higher when reaching for a ball than when I wasn't. I learned how to be the quickest in all of the fitness testing, by getting my leg in the right position to activate my glute muscle before taking off. I learned how to turn my body quicker than anyone else's by working out that if I turned my head first, it would spin my body around faster.

All of this hard work, and the lessons I was learning, were paying off on the court. I was quicker, and jumping higher allowed me to get loads more tips and intercepts. I felt almost invincible. For the first time, I was truly backing myself.

By the end of my first year with the Thunderbirds, we had improved my vertical jump by 15 centimetres, which is a lot for a lanky girl. Going from a 47-centimetre jump to a 62-centimetre jump was outrageous and made a huge difference to my game. Jamaican Goal Shooter Romelda Aiken is 196 centimetres tall and I am 187 centimetres, so if we could both jump the same height initially, that extra 15 centimetres gave me a greater reach than her. This meant that if I was ever to be back in my old position of Goal Keeper, I could potentially jump and intercept any ball that was thrown to her, even if it was placed correctly. Now that I knew how satisfying and fulfilling it was when the hard work paid off, I just wanted to get better and better.

But the pressure I was putting on myself to stay skinny and fit was starting to get out of control. I felt no guilt after eating healthy foods, but if I ate anything like chocolate or ice cream, I made myself throw it up afterwards. I knew this behaviour wasn't right, but I couldn't stop myself doing it. My performances on court were only encouraging this bad behaviour. People constantly told me how fit I was looking, and congratulating me on my weight loss, so I started seeing it as a positive thing.

I was hungry all the time but I was managing to make it through training sessions and games with enough energy, so I didn't worry too much about that. Being hungry all the time was just part of losing weight, I told myself. This was true, of course, but I became addicted to that feeling. If I wasn't feeling hungry, I worried that I was eating too much. I didn't want hunger to affect my training, so I made sure I had a protein bar before and after, but I stopped eating carbs and sugar altogether. I was trying to hide it as I didn't want people thinking I was too obsessive, so if they offered me ice cream or lollies I'd eat it in front of them, then throw it up afterwards.

I was hiding it from people in my private life, too, but that was easy as I didn't have a lot of time to see people outside of netball or my job at the solar company. Not long after arriving in Adelaide, I met a guy and we started going out. He was a firefighter and had to move to Darwin soon after we got together, but we decided to stick it out and do the long-distance thing. I only saw him once a month, if that, so it was easy to hide my bad habits from him. Good friends like Katie and Bec came to see me whenever they could, but their visits were brief and few and far between. This meant that they couldn't see what I was doing with my food either. The only one I had to be careful around was my housemate, Jas, but I managed to keep it hidden from her, too. I knew that what I was doing was wrong but as I seemed to be getting away with it, I kept it up. What harm could it be doing?

A lot, as it would turn out.

I was loving my Thunderbirds teammates and couldn't wait to get out on the court with them every week. They were a talented, hard-working and committed bunch of girls, but they liked having fun, too. One week, four of my teammates – Mo'onia, Kate, Georgia and Geva – told our coach, Jane, that they were going to stay on in Perth after our game instead of heading back to Adelaide. We had a bye the following week so Jane agreed they could stay in Perth for a bit longer. The four of them had actually ducked off to Bali for a mini holiday, keeping their cheeky getaway a secret. Or so they thought. The week after our bye we played in Sydney and Jane was being interviewed on a live TV show.

'And how do you feel about your players going to Bali mid-season, Jane?'

The shit hit the fan.

Everyone in the team was interrogated and asked if we knew about the holiday, which we didn't. I later found out that Mon had suspected me of dobbing them in, but I had absolutely no clue about their trip. From then on, they were dubbed 'The Bali Four'. Their holiday had no impact on their playing, or on the rest of the team, though, because in July the Thunderbirds made it to the Grand Final.

The build-up was the most exciting part of the whole thing. The city of Adelaide really got behind us and the sport. We were on billboards all over town, on the front page of the newspaper every day and did stacks of interviews. It was my first experience of the media in sport and I loved it. The week leading up to the big game, I was awarded 'Rookie of the Year', which not only earned me an esteemed title, but also a giant cheque for $5000. I felt like Happy Gilmore! Finally, I could pay off my car, which had been a huge weight on my shoulders when I wasn't earning a lot of money.

By the time the morning of the Grand Final arrived, I was pumped and ready to go! We had a sold-out crowd of ten thousand people at the Adelaide Entertainment Centre – the biggest crowd I'd ever played in front of – and the feeling of walking out on that court with them all going crazy was amazing. It was also my first full game that year, and I was totally in the zone, focused and confident, for all four quarters. I could feel that

I was playing well, so my confidence gathered momentum as the game went on. I was on fire!

With only five minutes left in the game we were ten goals up and I knew we'd won, but I had to keep going, even though all I wanted to do was jump up and down and hug my teammates. It was the hardest and longest five minutes of netball I've ever played. When the siren finally sounded, we all ran towards each other and went crazy. I found myself sandwiched between two of my heroes, Mo'onia Gerrard and Geva Mentor, and it all seemed so surreal. I had never dreamed I would meet these amazing sportswomen, let alone win a bloody Grand Final with them!

Winning that game meant so much more to me than getting a big trophy. It meant everything. After so many years of sitting on the bench, feeling completely worthless in comparison to my teammates, I finally knew what it felt like to be part of it all. Now I was the one who got to go out on that court, week after week, and show people what I could do. Sharing in the joy of a Grand Final win with my teammates, and knowing I'd truly earned my spot there and contributed to the game, was an amazing feeling. And to think how close I'd been to quitting netball at the start of the year. Within only six months I'd had such an amazing breakthrough in my training and my attitude, thanks to the incredible people around me, and I could finally reap the rewards of all my hard work and effort.

So yeah, that Premiership win meant everything to me. And to top an excellent week off, I received an email telling me I'd made the Australian Squad. The actual *friggin'* Open Australian Squad!

It was official. I was now considered one of the top twenty netballers in Australia.

But as is often the case in life, after the high highs come the low lows. Our Mad Monday, Crazy Tuesday and Party Wednesday celebrations were so wild that I was too sick to trial for the 2010 Commonwealth Games at the Australian Selection Camp in Canberra that weekend. I'd been drinking for three days straight and, after not having a single drink for six months, it messed with me and I came down with a really bad flu.

I found out later that, had I trialled, I had a good chance of making that Commonwealth Games team. Bizarrely enough I wasn't too bothered about missing the trials at the time as I didn't think I had a chance of making the team. Swings and roundabouts!

In the meantime, I was still dealing with other issues. Even though I couldn't trial, I still had to do all the non-physical tests, which included having my skinfolds done again. I had indeed dropped below 100mm, as had been my goal, but I'd gone much further than hitting 80mm. My skinfolds had dropped to 65mm, and the dieticians were thrilled.

'Well done, Sharni!'

They were happy that I'd committed to getting fitter, and as far as they were concerned, weight loss went hand in hand with that. I was now one of the skinniest girls on the team. The feedback I received for achieving this goal was, 'Great job!' which only solidified my belief that I was doing the right thing by throwing up the 'bad' foods. I want to make it clear that they in no way knew about this at any point in time. This was just how I personally received and perceived the feedback.

So, I kept doing it.

Since I hadn't made the Commonwealth Games team, I had

six months off. When you don't make the Australian team there's no choice as a netballer but to wait until the next preseason in December. As it turned out, I had enough to keep me distracted during these six months, although none of it was good.

I found out that my cousin was living in a drug rehab centre in Adelaide. My cousin and I are the same age and had always been close as kids, but we lost contact when he started going down the path of drugs in our teens. A lot of us in the family had given up on him – it was just too hard after a while – but when I found out that he was now in the same city as me I wanted to support him.

I started visiting him every week, trying to make up for lost time. He was supposed to stay in the centre for six months but after four months he called me one day.

'Hey, Cuz, I hate it in here,' he said. 'I want out. Can I come live with you?'

I was still living with Jas and so was hesitant about putting that kind of pressure on my friend.

'You need to do six months, mate.'

'Sharns, I'm leaving,' he said firmly. 'So either I move in with you or I go back to my old life.'

I didn't want him to go back to living with his druggie mates. I knew Jas wouldn't be happy but we had a spare bedroom, and he was family. Maybe if he was living with me, I could be a positive influence on him and get drugs out of his life forever?

My cousin moved in and from day one the atmosphere in the house changed and my friendship with Jasmine was strained. She tolerated him, but it ended up getting too hard and soon enough she ended up moving out. I was upset that things had turned out this way but I was still hopeful that I could turn things around for him and help get his life back on track.

I was wrong.

Soon after Jas moved out, my stuff started disappearing. Money, jewellery and other items. Gone. I confronted my cousin about this, but he denied taking anything, which I now know is all part of the illness. It was breaking my heart to see my cousin struggling with this horrible addiction. I could see that he wanted my love and my help, but ultimately I just didn't know how to help him get better or change the direction of his life. We were the same age, twenty-two, and I just didn't know what to do.

After a few months, I came home to find him completely stoned off his head. It was the final straw.

'The lease is up,' I said to him. 'I'm moving out and you're not coming. You need to sort your shit out.'

The next day he packed his bags and left. In the whole time he'd been there he never paid me a single cent for rent, food or utilities, and on top of this had left me $5000 short. I wasn't earning any money from netball for the six months that I wasn't playing, so I was stressed out and devastated at the way things had turned out.

I knew that Jasmine was staying in a new house with our friend, Lil, and that they had a spare room, so I called her.

'Jas, it didn't work out with my cousin. Can I come and live with you and Lil?'

'Of course you can, Sharn.'

My beautiful friend opened her arms to me, proving that she was my real family. I felt sick that I'd let her down and allowed my cousin to come between us. I was so blessed to have a friend like Jas in my life.

As for my cousin, I didn't hear from him. Not for years. To this day he still breaks my heart. But what do you do? That experience taught me that if people don't want to help themselves, there's nothing you can do, no matter how hard you try.

Life is about choice, and unfortunately, not everyone makes the right ones.

CHAPTER SEVENTEEN

ADELAIDE, PART TWO: DEFENDERS ARE MONGRELS

At the start of 2011 there was a huge exodus from the Adelaide Thunderbirds. Kate Beveridge (Goal Shooter) went back to Perth, Mo'onia Gerrard (Goal Defence) went home to New South Wales, and Geva Mentor (Goal Keeper) headed to Melbourne. Three of 'The Bali Four' were now gone.

Jane brought in a lot of talented young players, and I was promoted to Vice-Captain. The worst part of this new year was Jasmine having her contract revoked two weeks before the season started. It came totally out of the blue and she was devastated. I was so upset. There was no excuse for the way she'd been treated. A contract should be seen through and I was appalled at the way things went down. Within two weeks of getting this news, Jas was gone – she didn't have a job and moved to Canberra to live with her boyfriend – so it was just Lil and I left in the house.

With so many of our experienced players gone, the Thunderbirds had an influx of new, younger players, which meant not much was expected from us. No-one thought the Thunderbirds would win any games, let alone a Premiership, and it was nice to play games with no pressure for a little while. This lack of faith also meant that many teams underestimated us, so we ended up doing quite well. With Geva gone, I was put back in my original position of Goal Keeper. After playing Wing Defence for my whole first year at the club, I was anxious and excited to put my vertical jump training into effect against the VERY tall (196 centimetres) Jamaican Goal Shooter, Romelda Aiken. I was nervous, as I had lost some fitness after slipping a disc in my back during the offseason. But after four months of rehab, I managed to get back on track and was ready to roll for the season and to play against someone who would become my favourite opponent.

It's an intimidating thing to walk onto a court and stand next to an opponent whose elbow is at the same height as your nose. One sharp elbow to the schnoz can easily bend it sideways, which happened many times during my career. I've had it straightened twice already and am looking forward to my post-sport-career nose job.

Romelda's hands reach right up to the ring when she jumps, so defending her is hard work. There's nothing more frustrating than working your arse off, centre pass after centre pass, only to have a ball fly straight over the top of your head. Before increasing my vertical jump, I usually wouldn't have been able to get anywhere near the ball when playing against Romelda. But all that training I'd done the year before and the extra 15 centimetres I now had on my jump made a huge difference. The first time I jumped in the air and ripped an intercept no-one expected me to make, it was the best feeling in the world.

I was also still working with my sports psychologist and friend, Jenny Williams. Our bond had grown during our first year of working together, and Jenny was the one responsible for taking my game to a whole new level. I didn't discuss my eating disorder with her though, as I was too embarrassed, but I assumed she'd soon figure out that something wasn't right. She'd noticed how much my body had changed since arriving in Adelaide a year earlier.

'Sharni, you're too skinny,' she'd say to me.

I brushed her comments away and changed the subject. I was getting so many positive comments from everyone else about how great I looked that I wasn't going to worry about one person's opinion. Even if that person was someone who cared about my health and was the only one telling me the truth.

Jenny was a brilliant psychologist, and friend, and her number one priority when working with a team is making sure that everyone looks out for each other. She taught me how to 'Tigger' (bounce back quickly) after a poor performance or a bad game, saying that 'Eeyores' weren't good for sport. There was no point in moping after a game, as it only made you play worse in the next one.

She made me watch videos of my netball and sporting heroes, read books and watch movies, then tell her what I'd learned. Jenny also introduced me to the ten-thousand-hour mastery rule. She made me work out how many hours I'd put into training and playing over the years. I assumed I'd be well over the ten-thousand-hour mark, but I was only three-quarters of the way there. I still had a long way to go before hitting my Mastery of Netball goal, and this thought excited me. Jenny was as much a life coach as a psychologist and friend. She was always there when I needed her, as was her husband, Mark, and their daughter, Ellen. These people were like family to me, and once again I had to pinch myself at how lucky I'd been to make these special connections in life. To the point where when I accidentally chopped off the top of my thumb one night with a vegetable peeler, I walked down to their house so Dr Mark could stitch it back up for me in his living room. Life savers.

I was still working at the solar company but was starting to think about what else I might want to do with my life. When I was in high school, I'd listen to Tracy Bartram on the radio and think, 'I'd love to do that one day.' So, in 2011, I took the leap and signed up to do a broadcasting course at the Australian Radio School in Adelaide. I had no idea how I'd get a gig in radio after I finished studying, but at least I was taking that first important step.

The next thing I did was start harassing Triple M radio station about giving me a gig on their afternoon show. After a *lot* of badgering, they finally gave me a five-minute slot as the Work Experience Girl – a segment where I could talk about anything I wanted. I had to come up with ten ideas each week, and they would pick three for me to talk about on the radio once a week.

Around this time, I met Jodie Oddy, who worked at Mix FM Adelaide. When she found out that I was keen to get into radio she got me a job as the Mix FM competition girl, out on the road, five mornings a week. I couldn't believe it – my first proper job in radio!

I rocked up for my first day on the job at 5am on a cold winter's morning. Just before heading off in the Mix FM car, I looked down and saw that I was still wearing my ugg boots.

I called the boss.

'Um, hi, Chris?'

'Hi Sharni, you all good to go?'

'Well, kind of, but I was so excited to get to work today that I forgot to put shoes on. I'm wearing ugg boots.'

'Are you serious?'

'I'm serious.'

He sighed down the phone and I was suddenly terrified that I was about to lose this dream job on my first day.

'Okay, well, just don't get out of the car today,' he said.

'Thanks, Chris!'

I don't know when or where I came up with the belief that situations are only as awkward as you make them, but it's something I've lived by for as long as I can remember. Maybe I came up with it because I was always doing awkward things like this, completely accidentally. I think I developed the mantra as a way of accepting myself and my imperfections.

But after that first morning, I never forgot to put shoes on for work again.

My boyfriend was still living in Darwin, but he had applied for the South Australian firies so he could move back and be closer to me. Everything began slotting into place with my career and it felt like my relationship was on track, too. We'd been together for over a year at this point, and even though he was ten years older than me, it didn't seem to be a problem. Not while he was in Darwin anyway. But when he moved back to Adelaide for his recruitment course and asked if he could move in with me, I was hesitant. I loved going out with my mates and living the life of a young, independent woman. I was worried that my life as I knew it, and my freedom, would change too much if he moved in. He understood and agreed to move into his parents' house while he was doing the course.

The 2011 season had wrapped up, and as we were a young team we didn't make finals, which was to be expected. However, I played well enough in GK to earn my position back in the Australian Squad for the second year in a row. It was a big year for the Australian Team and world netball with the Netball World Cup taking place in Singapore in a few months' time. I was so excited to be a part of the squad, let alone to be trialling for an actual Netball World Cup. They only happen every four years, so making the Australian team in a World Cup year is a big deal. It's basically the Olympics of netball. Through a series of trial matches, twelve players are chosen out of a squad of twenty-two girls. I had spent the past year racking up more court time, playing full games, so I was really starting to enjoy playing against the more experienced players and was starting to hold my own. At trials, you often play in your top two positions, however because I also knew how to play well in Wing Defence, I was able to trial for all three positions, Goal Keeper, Goal Defence and Wing Defence. I felt no fear at the trials either, because I honestly didn't think I was going to make the team, I just wanted to give all of the girls I played against a really good run for their money.

And I absolutely killed it.

After the trials, we were all brought into a room to hear who made the team. As the names were read out in alphabetical order, I told myself that I'd given my best, so it didn't matter if I missed out. I remembered how awkward it had felt last year when they passed L, and I didn't hear my name. I was mentally preparing myself for the same thing to happen as they got closer to my letter.

J... K...
'Sharni Layton.'
That's me! I'm Sharni Layton!

I wanted to jump up and down but had to hold it in. It's an awkward process because once your name is announced, you have to sit and wait for everyone to be read out. After the last name they say 'that is all', then whoever misses out has to stand up and leave the room. They'd all congratulate you before leaving, but no-one wanted to get excited in front of them because you felt for them. Thank God they don't run trials like this anymore.

After a quick celebration with my selected teammates, I immediately called Mum, Dad and Kara.

'I'm in the Australian team!' I shouted down the phone. 'I'm going to a World Cup!'

Mum burst into tears, Dad laughed in his jovial excited way, while Kara screamed down the phone with me. None of us could believe it. There was a flurry of excited activity afterwards. Before the announcement was made public, I had to try on the uniform, get photos taken with the team and go on a tour of Prime Minister Julia Gillard's residence in Canberra. Unfortunately, Julia herself couldn't be there, but her partner Tim Mathieson met and greeted us. I was beside myself with excitement.

It was all so surreal. Especially when I could still vividly remember sitting in the nosebleeds at Melbourne Arena six years earlier, watching the Australian team play and thinking I would never be good enough to play at that level. Yet, here I was, about to don the green-and-gold dress and play for my country. I was officially one of the top twelve players in Australia.

Chelsea Pitman and Erin Bell were also picked as debutantes. It was wonderful to be able to share the excitement with two girls who'd been such a big part of my netball journey. Erin had played in Adelaide with me, and I'd known Chelsea since I was fifteen when I played in my first state tournament in Perth. Our vibrant energy filtered throughout the entire team, and the older girls embraced our excitement. Our happiness reminded them of their first time making the team, and of what netball was all about – fun and passion for the game.

CHAPTER EIGHTEEN

THE 2011 WORLD CUP

It's tradition that an older player presents a new player with their Australian team dress before their first game, and Natalie von Bertouch, the Thunderbirds Captain, presented me with mine. Receiving it from Nat was such an honour, especially since she was a huge part of why I was there in the first place. Nat had nurtured and supported me ever since I'd moved to Adelaide. After the game, Chelsea Pitman and I ran straight back to our rooms to put the dresses on and take photos of each other. Our very own Australian dresses ... with *our names on the back!* Seeing myself in that uniform for the first time was a moment I'd never forget.

We played two games in New Zealand before heading to Hong Kong for a camp and then Singapore for the Netball World Cup. Before each game, we would meet in a room at our hotel to hear the coach announce who would be playing in the team that day, then hop on a bus to head to the match. Game two came around and we were listening to our coach, Norma Plummer, read out the team.

'Starting Wing Defence, Sharni Layton.'

What? *Shit!*

My very first game playing for Australia – *and I was starting!*

Mo'onia Gerrard was usually the starting Wing Defence, but she walked straight over and patted me on the shoulder.

'Go get 'em, kid!'

That meant the world to me, as did the opportunity Norma had given me. I was going to do everything I could to stay focused and play my best now that I had the support of my hero, too.

That first game was wild. I thought the ANZ Championship had a crazy intensity, but this was next level. I was playing on Temepara Bailey (nee George) one of the world's best and feistiest Wing Attacks at that time. She ran rings around me, and I couldn't believe that after all my preparation, I still had to step it up so much to keep up at this level. I was dragged at half-time, but I came off knowing I'd given it my all. I knew it was fair enough that I'd been taken off when I wasn't keeping up with my player. I'd have to put in a lot more work to be great at this level of the competition.

We lost our first game by one or two goals, but it's not a bad thing to lose before the World Cup because it teaches you what you need to improve on. I was grateful that Norma had backed me and allowed me to learn that lesson. Not many other coaches had done this in my experience.

After the New Zealand games, we travelled to Hong Kong for a training camp, then on to Singapore for the World Cup. I'd never been anywhere like Hong Kong and it blew my mind. I was in awe of the high-rise buildings and the buzzing, crowded atmosphere down on the streets. It was crazy!

This was a busy time for us as a team, but we also had plenty of downtime to do some shopping and sightseeing when we weren't training. I was enjoying finding my way in the Australian team, and how I fitted in. Norma was a tough coach and tough on all of her players, but we had a good relationship based on our history together. Norma had lived in Canberra and worked out of the AIS when I was staying there, and we'd had many conversations about horses, elephants and other non-netball related topics. I felt comfortable around her. I could be open and honest, and she felt the same way about me.

When you're on tour, every player has multiple check-ins with the coach. It's a chance to let the coach know how you're feeling, and for them to tell you how they think you're going and what you need to improve on. We had a lot of downtime in Hong Kong, so it was a perfect opportunity for Norma to catch up with everyone. When my turn came around I was nervous to hear how she thought I was going. I was new to the team so she'd been hard on me at training when I stuffed up the game plan or wasn't training at a high enough intensity. I was trying to learn as fast as I could but was finding it hard. This was my opportunity to talk to her about it in a relaxed environment.

'Sharni, what's going on?' she asked. 'How are you finding camp?'

I decided to be straight with her. 'Norma, I know you have high expectations of me, which I love, but if you give me too much to work on at once, I'll get confused. That's when I train poorly.'

'Go on.'

'If you give me one thing to fix, I'll nail it,' I said. 'If you give me two things, I'll do them okay. If you give me three things, I'll touch on all of them, but I won't do them well. And if you give me any more than that, I'll get confused and do absolutely nothing.'

She took everything I said on board, and it was a relief. I was proud of myself for speaking up. It was such a good feeling to have reached a point in my career where I could be honest with my coach. Not only that, but I was also finally able to acknowledge and articulate my strengths and weaknesses as a player.

I had finally figured out how I ticked. It had taken all these years and all these experiences for me to learn and gain the confidence to verbalise my feelings of unease with the Australian Coach herself. I'd grown so much since my days at the Kestrels and the Vixens, but I was also so grateful to Norma for making me feel safe enough to open up to her.

After this, Norma knew exactly how to get the most out of me as a player. A lot of people saw Norma as a hard-arse, but I knew how much she cared. Jenny taught me that caring is one of the most important qualities a coach can possess, and Norma has this quality in spades.

When our team finally arrived in Singapore, it was time to rock. We'd put in all the hard work, and now we had to seal the deal and win this World Championship. We played lots of games in the lead-up and I got a good run against Sri Lanka, Jamaica and Malawi. Most of us were put on the court across all the games, which kept the morale of the group up. Erin, Chelsea and I were just so happy to be there that we probably wouldn't have cared if we got many games or not.

The atmosphere was electric. I'd never experienced anything like it. Thousands of Aussies had travelled to Singapore for the games, dressed up in wigs and all their green-and-gold glory. They'd made signs for their favourite players and would continually chant and sing during the games. Our fans created an incredible vibe, and I loved how they energised me.

Mum and Dad were there, too, but Kara was running her hairdressing salon and couldn't afford to take time off. She was sorry she couldn't be there but checked in with me every day. All of the team's families would go out for dinner together at night, and we all had a great time travelling to and from the games together, too.

The Aussie team won all of our round games. When we came up against Jamaica in the Semi-Final, we beat them to earn our place in the World Cup Final the next day. New Zealand had beaten England to earn their spot and, as history would have it, Australia and New Zealand were facing off for the World Championship. New Zealand had beaten Australia the year before in overtime at the Delhi Commonwealth Games, so we were ready to take back the number one spot.

The game didn't disappoint. It was tight to the wire, and when the final whistle blew it was a draw. Just like the year before, the game went into overtime. I was exhausted just watching from the side. I didn't know how the girls on the court were doing it. All five of us on the bench used every inch of energy we had to yell and scream encouragement to our teammates.

Overtime consists of two seven-minute halves of play, changing ends after the first half. When Caitlin Bassett took a shot at goal ONE SECOND before the final buzzer, the ball went through the ring and we had won by one goal! We jumped up, screamed and launched ourselves at each other in the biggest stacks-on ever seen, simultaneously laughing and crying.

We were WORLD CHAMPIONS!

Popping champagne in the change rooms, we took a moment to bask in our glory, and in each other. After having a million photos taken with the trophy, we headed back to our hotel to change and attend a post-match Netball Australia function. It was a top night. We all hit the Singapore clubs before saying a sad goodbye to each other the next day. We'd spent three weeks together, working towards this amazing achievement, and now we were going home to our own cities. I wanted the experience, and the feeling, to last forever, but of course it never does.

There are no words to describe the elation I felt after winning a World Cup. Of having achieved something I had never thought would be possible for me. To be in a team who would forever be part of netball history. I was there!

I was part of something magical.

CHAPTER NINETEEN

BACK TO PLANET EARTH

When I returned home after the whirlwind experience of the World Cup, I realised that I wasn't enjoying my job at the solar place anymore. Each of us in the Australian netball team had been given a nice monetary bonus for winning the Cup, so I took the opportunity to quit my job and take another trip. Although this one would be very different from the trip I'd just had.

Emma, the Thunderbirds team chaplain, was heading to the Philippines to do missionary work in local communities. When she asked me if I wanted to go with her, I didn't hesitate. I wanted to use my time off from netball to do something meaningful and this was perfect. Also, my family was sponsoring a child through World Vision, named Saretha, who lived in Cambodia, so I'd be able to visit her, too.

We flew to Cambodia first and Emma came with me to meet Saretha and her community. I took a suitcase full of old uniforms and netballs to give out to the kids there, and I couldn't wait to meet Saretha and her family and see her village. But the experience was nothing like what I had expected.

From the moment I arrived, it felt like the people in the village were trying to impress me, when all I'd wanted was to experience the community as it really was and spend time with Saretha and her mum. It made me a bit sad. I wanted to take every single one of them out to a supermarket and stock up on food, but they insisted on going out to lunch instead. I left feeling deflated and useless, and like I hadn't done nearly as much as I should have.

Emma and I continued to the Philippines, where we had much more of an opportunity to give back to a community. I learned how much more helpful it was to put time and effort into a community than just donate money to a charity organisation. Emma's church did a fantastic job supporting the people there, and we were able to help out in drug rehab centres and the poor communities in Cebu.

We also visited an isolated community in the hills where the kids loved the balls and gifts I gave out. We met a teacher who was there training other teachers in the community, an engineer who was setting up water tanks, and medics who were tending to the community's health needs. I felt so honoured to be on this trip and to meet these amazing people who were doing such good with their lives. The experience made me appreciate the life I was so lucky to have, but I also gained a lot of perspective. The people in these impoverished communities were so happy and grateful for the little they had in their lives. They had it all figured out and knew that having each other mattered above all else. They didn't sweat the small stuff like we do.

I returned to Adelaide in 2012 with a renewed sense of self and appreciation for my life, and the year started well. I began working at a dog daycare centre and loved it. There was no better job than spending all day with animals as far as I was concerned.

When I was named Co-Captain of the Thunderbirds, alongside Nat von Bertouch, it was a huge honour. In just three years I'd worked my way up to becoming a leader at a club that I loved. I was feeling happy and confident about being somewhere I felt I truly belonged.

But things on the personal front weren't going so well. My boyfriend was still living with his family in Adelaide but had been acting differently towards me since I'd returned from the World Cup. I assumed he was still shitty because I hadn't let him move in with me, and because I'd gone off travelling around the world without him. *Come on, mate!* I thought. *You need to get over it!*

But when he continued to grow more distant from me, I began to worry. We started arguing a lot and eventually reached breaking point. When he disappeared on me at a wedding I realised that I was done with being treated like shit. He just wasn't invested anymore, and when he came to see me the next day he told me it was over. I was heartbroken, I didn't know what I'd done wrong. It wasn't until a few weeks later I found out he had found love with his personal trainer at the Fire Recruitment Academy. When I learned the truth, it hurt even more. We'd been together for nearly two years at that stage. We'd spent the first eighteen months in a long-distance relationship, and he'd moved back to Adelaide to be closer to me, only to fall in love with someone else. He wanted to stay friends, but I cut all contact with him.

I decided to put all my focus on netball and my job, but the sadness and betrayal I felt after the break-up started impacting other areas of my life. No-one had yet noticed my eating disorder and with this new added stress, it went to the next level. Jenny was still telling me to eat more, because she noticed I had lost even more weight. I had cut back on eating altogether and started running. Soon, I was achieving personal bests, but this was only because I was training so much to distract myself from everything else going on. It was a low time. Working in dog daycare was keeping me sane, but the long hours there on top of my training schedule was tiring.

I was still doing media stuff. It didn't pay much but that didn't worry me because I knew it was important. For the first time in my life, I was being recognised on the streets in Adelaide. I figured that if people saw me on sports shows, and liked me, there was a good chance they'd come to our games. I wanted netball to be as big and popular on the main stage as AFL was. Our product was just as good, so I couldn't understand why it hadn't happened sooner.

But, to my dismay, my media work started to have a negative impact on my relationships at the club. I don't know if it was jealousy at play, or if they just thought I was distracted, but I started copping criticism. No-one ever criticised me directly, but I started hearing things from people at the club like, *'Do you know the coach is mad at you about such and such?'* and *'Do you know this teammate doesn't like this about you?'*

It was frustrating to know things were being said behind my back. No-one ever came to me directly to ask why I was working in the media, or why I was doing what I was doing. Judgements were just whispered around me. I began to withdraw from my team and kept on with my media work without talking to anyone about it, especially not my coach.

I didn't want her thinking I wasn't serious about netball, which seemed to be people's perception from the whispers I was hearing about how I was being portrayed. I found it bizarre that my teammates worked at hospitals, or as teachers, or in cafes, and those jobs weren't seen as distractions, yet mine was. My relationship with my coach began to deteriorate and it seemed that I was always getting in trouble for one thing or another. For some reason we weren't communicating the way we had in the first two years at the club and it felt like I was constantly walking on eggshells.

Unfortunately, at the time when I felt like I was being pushed up against a wall, my instinct was to rebel. I just got louder and pushed the limits further, and this kind of behaviour only frustrated my coach even more.

As far as I was concerned, I was just being myself and this was getting me into trouble. I felt like a misfit, not for the first time in my life, and was miserable every time I was around the netball courts and at the club.

Carla Borrego was a teammate who didn't exactly comply either, and she copped a lot of heat as a result. As outsiders, we empathised deeply with one another and became good friends. Having one other kept us sane.

Then I hurt my shoulder.

The Thunderbirds were playing a friendly against the men's team, when my tough-nut assistant coach, Dan Ryan, rammed me. After an examination, I was told I'd subluxed (partially dislocated) my shoulder and torn my rotator cuff and was sent straight to the surgeon. He confirmed that I needed surgery, but left the decision to the club and me about whether or not I wanted to do it straight away or wait until the end of the season. I decided I wanted to play the rest of the season out.

Despite my shoulder injury, I was still playing good netball. We made Finals but fell short in the Semi-Final against a New Zealand side. All in all, it had felt like a pretty average year for me, especially after the highs of 2011, and by the end of the Thunderbirds season, all I wanted was to play with the Australian team again. Despite knowing I would have to get my shoulder fixed eventually, I decided to go to camp and play it down as much as I could.

On my first day at the Australian Team Camp, the Australian team's physio, an old friend of mine, took one look at me and frowned.

'Sharni, your shoulder is weak' he said 'if you continue to play, you risk doing more damage. It's your call but I recommend that you get it fixed as soon as possible'.

I knew what he was saying, but I didn't want to hear it.

'I've just played five games, what's another three before I get it fixed?'

He explained that it could be a lot longer and harder recovery if something else was to go wrong and he didn't think it would be worth it, but left the ball in my court. I knew what I had to do but it was devastating.

I'd been looking forward to playing with the Australian team all year and didn't want to be one of those players who was constantly in and out of the team. I'd worked so hard to get there and wanted to be able to properly make my mark. I cried for days.

There was another problem, too: money. Neither the Thunderbirds nor the Australian team's insurance would cover the cost of the surgery or months of rehab, which was around $7000. Although the injury had occurred while I was playing for the Thunderbirds, by the time I decided to have surgery I was no longer in contract. This meant that the insurance companies associated with the team wouldn't cover the costs. The Australian team's insurance wouldn't pay for it either because I hadn't made the team. I had no pay slips to give the insurance company and was unable to work, with no financial compensation to cover me.

Stuck in the middle, I had no choice but to ask my parents to put up the money for the surgery and rehab costs. It was a big ask and I felt terrible taking money from them. On top of this, I couldn't afford to live in Adelaide. I was contracted for 2013 but that season didn't start until December and it was July, so I had to go home to Melbourne and move back in with Mum and Dad.

The whole experience made it clear to me that the system needed to change. So, all through the off-season I worked with the Players' Association to have a new insurance clause put in the CBA (Collective Bargaining Agreement). The CBA determined all players' pay and leave, but there was nothing in there about the clubs covering insurance if a player is injured when training for the club outside of their contract period. I wanted to change that. We worked hard to make it happen and, after a long six months, we succeeded. The new clause covered mental health as well as physical injuries and I was so proud when it finally went through. I was paid out by Netball Australia Insurance eventually and I do have to give Netball Australia a huge shout out, as they were incredibly supportive throughout the whole process.

During my six months back in Melbourne, I started rehab with the Vixens trainer. It was all going well until I rolled my ankle during one of our sessions and suddenly, I was immobile. After years of non-stop training, travelling and playing sport, I was stuck on the couch in my parents' house, separated from my teammates and friends. I couldn't even ride my horse.

All of this started to take a toll on my mental health, but I was determined not to let it get me down. Thanks to a good friend, Aiden Blizzard, who was looking out for me, I looked at a life-coaching course he had recently completed. I didn't know what to expect but it ended up being *exactly* what I needed. I learned so much about myself and my personality, which made me see that the complications I'd been having with my coach in Adelaide were very likely caused by my negative attitude. To try to make sure these problems wouldn't arise again, I planned to apply several reframing techniques that would help me approach life with the Thunderbirds from a more positive place.

While in Melbourne, I met a guy named Nic and we started going out. Unlike the firefighter, Nic was younger than me, but we got along and had fun, so when I moved back to Adelaide at the start of 2013, he came, too.

We moved to Glenelg and it was nice to be around someone who was so chilled and fun. I knew it was a big leap to move in with someone I'd only been with for a short time, but I figured I'd give it a go and see what happened.

Soon after I started back training with the Thunderbirds, it became clear that the coach and I still weren't getting along. Despite my new attitude of trying to see things from her point of view, I realised there was very little I could do to change things between us. It seemed that she wasn't a fan of my new boyfriend, suggesting he was too immature for me. I couldn't understand why anyone would have an opinion on who I went out with, as my relationship with him had nothing to do with my spot in the team. I just wished everyone would stay the hell out of my personal life, whether it was my boyfriend, my media work or what I ate for breakfast; I just wanted to be left alone and only judged for my performances on the court, which mattered most.

I decided to do whatever it took to get through the year without too much trouble, but this turned out to be a lot harder than it sounded, especially when I was being prevented from attending my best friend's wedding during preseason in February.

Bec and I had mutual friends at school but we didn't connect until after Year Twelve finished when she went on a GAP program in Vanuatu for six months. We started writing letters to each other while she was away, and our bestie love blossomed. When she got back from Vanuatu we were extremely close, and even though we lived interstate from each other most of our friendship, we talked almost every day.

I told the club that if they wouldn't let me fly back to Melbourne for Bec's wedding, I'd drive. I had sacrificed so many important events over the years, but I wasn't prepared to miss my best friend's wedding. I also knew that another player in the team had been allowed to fly back and forth from Sydney, and to leave training sessions early to get home interstate for a night. I had no issue with this, but I did have an issue with rules applying to some but not to others.

Bec was a hugely important part of my life. She had asked me to be her bridesmaid and to speak during the ceremony. It was preseason, which meant I wouldn't be missing any training, so I didn't understand why I couldn't go. The only reason I had asked for permission was that I was trying to do the right thing and show my new positive attitude. On reflection, I probably shouldn't have asked at all. I went to Bec's wedding anyway, which didn't go down well at all.

Soon after this, I was told there would be no leadership position for me in 2013 as my attitude wasn't in line with the club's values. I'd gone from being Team Captain to having no leadership role in one year and it stung, but I didn't argue with the decision because there was no point. If this was their view, I knew there was nothing I could say that would change things. Arguing my case would only make things worse. I knew my relationship with the club had deteriorated after I fought to be reimbursed for the shoulder surgery that Netball Australia ended up covering, even though I never hounded them about it. I couldn't figure out why I was such a 'bad guy' in the club's eyes and felt like opening my mouth would make it worse. Sometimes it's just a lose-lose situation, as it seemed like every time I tried to fix a situation it was used against me in another way.

But losing the leadership role helped in a way. I now felt I had no responsibility to the team, I went back to turning up to training, doing what I had to do, and leaving. Carla and I continued to stick together, we confided in each other and I felt bad I hadn't supported her more while I was in those leadership roles. I'd been completely unaware of the shit she'd been going through in her years with the club, as I was in my happy bubble at the time and thought everything was rosy. But once I started expressing myself, I found myself on the outer, too, and this is where I was lucky to have Carla on my side and as my friend. We had games nights and dinners together, along with our partners, to keep life fun.

We needed this stuff to keep us sane, especially when we felt like we were constantly getting in trouble for something or another.

I'd get in trouble for turning up to training in ugg boots during winter, and for wearing a hat in summer.

Just as I didn't think things could get any worse, the team doctor called me in and told me, without completing a mental health assessment of any kind, that I had depression. I was still seeing Jenny Williams, my psychologist, at the time and knew this wasn't true. I was just sad about the way I was being treated by my coach and the club, as anyone who wasn't getting along with their boss or co-workers would.

The club decided they didn't like Jenny, so I was being forced to see an external psychiatrist and made to have fortnightly meetings with Emma, the team chaplain. Emma was my friend, and we had travelled together, but things became increasingly weird between us when I was forced to have these sessions with her. But I was told in no uncertain terms that I wouldn't be allowed to play if I didn't go to these, and the psychiatrist's, meetings.

My Adelaide dad, Tony, came with me to a meeting with the CEO and club doctor to explain that I shouldn't have to be forced to attend these sessions. While I refused to go to the psychiatrist, I was made to go see a different psychologist that had no connection with either party. It was seriously fucked. After every training session, I felt so low and confused, and I'd cry in the shower. I had been so happy to begin with in Adelaide, and had made some of the best friends of my life, but suddenly everything felt like it was falling apart.

Thankfully I had Nic and the Lunniss family to support me during this time. Nic, in particular, was great, and eventually helped me overcome my eating disorder when he caught me throwing up one day. After that, he held me accountable. He knew I always threw up after eating bad food, so he wouldn't let me binge the way I had before. I felt so ashamed about being busted and someone knowing my dirty little secret that I soon stopped. It was as if all I'd needed was for someone to notice what I was doing and tell me it was wrong. I had too much pride and was embarrassed to keep doing it.

Jenny taught me strategies to deal with what was happening at the club. For example, in the lead-up to games I'd do visualisations so that when the coach yelled at me non-stop during the match, I could block her out and not let it affect my performance. I used this same technique during training sessions.

But when the club told me I was banned from working in the media, I decided enough was enough.

It started when I got a call from my boss, Roo, at Triple M one day.

'Hey, Sharns, can you come on the show today?'

'Sure, Roo. Just call the club to let them know.'

A short while later, Roo called me back. 'Hey, Sharns, the club says you're not free. Can I ask a different player to come on?'

This was a lie, and it was the moment I saw how the club was trying to control every area of my life. It wasn't right. I didn't know why they were doing it, but I knew I had to remove myself from the negative environment I was in.

But what to do now? I knew I wanted to be happier, but I also wanted to become an even better defender and get a playing/starting spot in the Australian team. I wasn't done with my professional netball career just yet. No-one was going to keep me down!

I had to find a new team, so I got on the phone and started chasing other offers and other teams. Jenny helped me put a series of questions together for each team I approached so I wouldn't find myself in the same situation down the track. She told me that I had to figure out what I didn't like about my current club, as well as what was important to me when joining a new club. These were the questions we came up with:

'What's your team culture like?'

'What do you think of my game?'

'How would I fit into your team?'

'Where and how can you help me improve?'

I also relied on the expert advice of others I trusted and respected, including Norma Plummer and Simone McKinnis, and together we weighed up my options. Perth was a long way away, and I'd learned over the years that I didn't like being too far away from my family and friends. Simone was keen to bring me back to Melbourne, but I still had a bad taste in my mouth after my younger years at the Vixens. Finally, I called Rob Wright, the head coach at the New South Wales Swifts. He was blunt.

'Sharni Layton, you are good,' he said, 'but you are not great. Your footwork needs a lot of work. If you come to Sydney, I'll work with you to make you the best defender in the world.'

I was sold.

Times you should apologise #19

When you spill eggs Benedict all over a customer while working a shift at the local cafe, and eat your wages' worth of food every week.

(SORRY, JAY)

CHAPTER TWENTY

GOAL KEEPERS DON'T YELL INSTRUCTIONS

I was twenty-six when I moved to Sydney, and the change in environment was the best thing for me. Within hours of arriving in the big smoke, I felt like I'd come home.

After being paid around $30,000 a year in Adelaide, I was now being paid more than four times that amount to play for the Swifts. This was a huge leap in my pay grade, and I was having trouble wrapping my head around it. It was almost a decade since I'd first signed with the Melbourne Kestrels, and now, here I was being paid properly to play the sport I had grown to love. I finally felt valued as a professional athlete in the world of netball.

Now that I was playing with the Swifts and being paid appropriately, I could focus 100 per cent on my training and recovery full-time, without having to get a part-time job to supplement my income, as I'd done for so many years. My time with the Thunderbirds had helped me develop into a good netballer, but now I was ready to become a *great* netballer. Being a great player had never come easy to me, and I knew I'd have to work my arse off. After my early years of riding the pine (bench-sitting), I was determined not to walk away from netball without knowing how good I could truly be.

I moved into a small one-bedder in Rozelle in Sydney's inner-west, and couldn't get over how expensive it was to rent in Sydney. Paying $550 per week for a one-bedder was out of control, but I wanted to be close to the city and make the most of living there.

Nic moved with me, even though we both knew our relationship was probably on its last legs. He'd been supportive of me in Adelaide and helped me with my eating disorder, but we weren't a good match. I'd been drawn to his chilled, fun personality in the beginning, but my eyes were now open to all the reasons why Nic wasn't good for me. He was a total sweetheart, but we had different driving forces. I needed someone to challenge and push me, and Nic wasn't that person. Also, I knew deep down that I wasn't in love with him. But for now, we got on with things and ignored the reality of how I felt.

I liked my new coach, Rob Wright, the moment I met him. Before I took the leap to move to Sydney, when he told me he'd make me the best defender in the world, my first thought was, *Bit cocky, isn't he?*

But I liked that he was willing to push me.

'If you move to Sydney, I promise I'll create a giant, larger-than-life papier-mâché Sharni Layton,' he'd said. (True to his word, in my second year at the club, my face was plastered on the billboard outside the stadium: a life-size papier-mâché Sharni Layton, just like he promised.)

I soon fell in love with the Sydney lifestyle, the new club and my new coach and teammates. It's hard to get *everything* right in a professional sporting job, or any job. You might have a great coach and team, but you don't always get to play. You might find a club you love playing for, but there are political issues within the organisation. Or you might have a great team, but there's a lack of leadership. You might get to play in every match, but don't get along with your teammates and disagree with the team culture. It is very rare, if not impossible, to tick every box, but for me, the Swifts were as good as it gets.

My game certainly improved under Rob's coaching, as well as my confidence, and I had a fantastic first season with my new team. Even though we lost our Semi-Final and were knocked out, I was rewarded with a spot in the Australian team for the 2014 Commonwealth Games, which was a huge achievement and a big bucket-list item.

Once I'd decided that netball *was* for me after making my first World Cup in 2011, I'd set my sights on the next Commonwealth Games and that time had finally come. I was nervous about the trials, but I was still playing three positions – Goal Keeper, Goal Defence and Wing Defence – which definitely worked to my advantage.

This was probably my favourite Australian team. My teammate Kim Green had become a great friend since moving to Sydney, and Bianca Chatfield and I had also become close after touring together in 2013. Bianca has the most positive attitude I have ever come across, and is my spirit sister. She has always empowered me. We used to sneak down to the team room after dinner, do yoga together and have life chats for hours on end. Being on tour was draining because you trained, ate, slept and talked netball for weeks on end. It was nice to have a little escape with Bianca.

We arrived in Glasgow for the Games. It was my first time staying in a village with other athletes, and was the closest I'd ever get to the Olympics. I was so excited. I was rooming with Caitlin Bassett, and as we both loved a sleep-in and are equally relaxed humans, it was a perfect match. We had our schedule down pat – alarm, quick shower, power-walk to breakfast, coffee on the way back, head off to the game. All within thirty minutes. Nailed it.

Some of our teammates were slightly more organised than us. Renae Ingles and Madi Browne roomed across from us, and when we finally woke from our slumber they'd already be dressed, with their hair and make-up done and their ankles strapped – all before my first morning wee.

The Commonwealth Games were fun, but also challenging. Despite playing Goal Keeper for years now, I was still in the Wing Defence position for the Australian team. Swinging back to a position I wasn't playing week in week out was becoming increasingly difficult. It was an even tougher gig considering the standard I needed to perform to and the fact I took the bib from my teammate Renae, the world's best Wing Defence.

Our coach, Lisa, changed the starting Wing Defence for every game, but even though Renae and I were both hugely competitive and vying for the same bib it didn't stop us supporting one another. Whenever I started in Wing Defence, Renae would give me all her notes and tell me what she'd do when playing against a specific Wing Attack player, and I'd do the same when she was starting. At break-time we'd talk through whatever challenges we were encountering with our opposition. Our last game of the round was against England, and they were winning. As far as I knew we'd never lost to England during tournament rounds, so I was on the edge of my seat (being on the bench for this particular game).

It's much easier to be able to see what's going on from the sidelines (a note for all you recliner-chair athletes out there who are happy to tell someone how a game should be played!). It's a completely different viewpoint when you're actually on the court and in the game. Netball is SO fast. The ball is released every second on the second and you have to figure out where it's going, then change direction and interpret where it's going in the next second, within a second.

This shit is intense!

Sitting on the bench watching the game, I could see that England had the mental edge over us and I wasn't going to have a bar of it. When three-quarter time came around, Lisa gave me the nod to go on and I knew what to do. I had to get inside my opposition players' heads and mess with their confidence, and that I did.

I roughed them up. I challenged every single ball my player, Serena, took, physically pushing her around (as much as I could without being called for contact) and it threw her off her game. Australia started taking back control of the game and we won by one goal, finishing on top of the table leading into Finals. Now, I'm not saying that win was down to me, but I was proud to have had a positive impact in an important match.

The Semi-Final match was close but this time it was Renae who saved the day, and I suspected she'd be starting in the Grand Final. We made a pact that no matter who was handed the WD bib for the Grand Final, the other would support them 100 per cent. We were playing for our country, not ourselves.

Renae was indeed handed the bib in the big game, and our team went on to smash New Zealand, winning by twenty-odd goals. It sucks to be a bench player in a Grand Final but over the years I'd learned to appreciate the role I played in a team, even when I wasn't on court. I knew I'd contributed to our win by bringing a positive attitude to a tough situation and helping us get over the line.

Mum came to Glasgow to support me and we'd decided to make the most of our time on the other side of the world. After the Games we headed straight to the Edinburgh Fringe Festival for some much-needed R and R.

A month before leaving for Glasgow, I found myself on a TV show with the comedian Jimeoin, and asked him if he'd be at the Edinburgh Festival. He said he would, so we exchanged numbers and made a plan to catch up. He kindly organised a bunch of tickets to his show for Mum, me and a bunch of others who'd come to the festival and put free drinks on the bar for us. Legend! He clearly knew the way into the hearts of athletes who'd just wrapped up a gruelling nine months of netball.

We loved Jimeoin's show and he joined us for dinner afterwards. Then Mum, Jimeoin and I powered on to a Fringe afterparty. At around 2am, Jimeoin asked if his mate could interview me. I agreed, and the next thing I knew there was a dictaphone in front of my face.

'Who are you?' he asked

'SHARNI FUCKING LAYTON!'

'And what have you just done, Sharni?'

'WE JUST WON A FUCKING GOLD MEDAL FOR AUSTRALIA!' To say I was pumped would be an understatement.

I had now achieved my dream of winning a World Cup and a Commonwealth Games after all. The whole experience of finally achieving your goals and dreams is so surreal.

He interviewed my mum, too, but I have no idea what she said. After a long and fun night, Kaz and I wrapped things up at about 5am, and when I woke the next morning I had a vague recollection of recording a podcast.

There are over two thousand comedians here, I thought. *There's no way that guy would have been a big deal.*

But when I turned on my phone, I saw that I'd been tagged in a Tweet, and it turned out that the dude who interviewed me had over seventy thousand followers.

I panicked. I knew I'd be in deep shit if that interview got out. It wasn't exactly the perfect-athlete response that the netball world encourages. But thankfully no-one who followed netball ever uncovered it.

Over the next week, Jimeoin took Kaz and me under his wing, showing us the city and taking us on walks. One day we saw a three-legged dog climbing up Arthur's Seat, puffing his little heart out.

'Let's give him some water,' Jimeoin said.

I put my hands out so he could fill them with water, as Mum forced the dog's head into my hands. And that's when it bit me, puncturing my finger. Mum and Jimeoin found it hilarious – but me, not so much. It bloody hurt!

The next day, we said our goodbyes to our new mate, Jimeoin, and headed off to Mum's beautiful homeland of Norway. On arrival, we headed straight to the hospital to get me a tetanus shot, and then we were ready to kick off our holiday.

We hiked mountains and took a cruise from the bottom of Norway, all the way to the top, through the fjords. My grandpa and great-grandpa were both seamen, so being on a boat felt like a good way to connect with my ancestors. Mum and I fell in love with the fjords. We took a speedboat ride through Bodo, kayaked in Tromso and enjoyed a Viking feast on them, too. It was so nice spending quality time with Mumma Kaz. I loved hearing about everything that was going on with my gorgeous mum, and just talking about life in general with her. We had a bottle of gin and tonic in our cabin and had brought our own cups, and we sipped away and caught up on everything we had missed since I moved interstate seven years earlier.

We cruised up to Hammerfest, the northernmost town in the world, where my cousin Jonas and his beautiful family live, and stayed with them for a few days. I loved hanging with my second cousins. The kids didn't speak English, and I didn't speak Norwegian, so we all communicated through Google Translate, which was hilarious. Otherwise, and as family should, we communicated through body language, hugging and caring for one another and making up for lost time. It was sad to leave, but they promised to come and visit us over the following couple of years, which they did, and our bond has grown even stronger.

Next we headed to Denmark, where my grandma grew up, and discovered the magic of Scandinavia. Mum and I ran around the Tivoli Amusement Park like twelve-year-olds and took walking tours around the city. It was in Denmark that I knew I had to start finding gyms to work out in. I'd had two weeks off training by then and needed to start running and doing weights for the upcoming Diamonds tour. Turns out that running around the streets is a great way to see a new city and country! I love how forward-thinking Scandinavia is with bike lanes bigger than the car lanes on the roads – how they look after the earth is next level. It puts Australia to shame, and I hope that we catch up soon before we do too much damage to this beautiful earth.

After Denmark, we went to France where we visited my old AIS/Thunderbirds mate, Jasmine. She'd been living there for two years with her husband, Peter. They lived in Grenoble, a stunning town surrounded by the Alps, and took us to beautiful restaurants and Annecy, where we parachuted off the Alps. Looking down at the lake from the air was an incredible experience, and for someone who had always been scared of heights, the experience changed me forever. It was so good to spend quality time with Jas, too, since we'd only seen each other once or twice a year since she'd left Adelaide.

After five weeks of amazing travel adventures, Mumma Kaz went home. I'd organised to meet up with Bianca and Kim in Bali on the way home, as a chance to reset and have our own mini training camp. We knew we had an Australian Camp coming up the following week, so we planned to have a dry week and get back on track. Well, we might have had a cocktail or two … but it was well balanced with multiple training sessions and a good daily sweat-up.

I arrived back in Sydney to discover that I had a bit more of a public profile and had been nicknamed 'The Enforcer' after my hard-arse attitude in the game against England. This wasn't the only attention I was receiving. There was a lot of recognition and reward that came with winning the tournament, and with a World Cup in Sydney the following year on the horizon, and a lot of sponsors started jumping on board. I had moved to Sydney at the perfect time; our sport was at its peak and I was at the forefront. I loved working in the media and doing ads and interviews. I was born for it. I love that I can be myself in front of a camera and get to share my dorky, yet strong and self-assured presence with Australia. It was what I had worked so hard for since I was in Adelaide, and I was starting to reap the rewards. It felt amazing. I couldn't believe I had started getting paid for doing what I loved.

Even though I wasn't a 'starting' player, I had become one of the most recognisable players on the team thanks to my booming voice and 'out there' personality. For the first time in my eleven-year career, the money started pouring in as I worked with brands like Samsung, Swisse, Elastoplast, Action Sports, Asics and 20Four. What I loved about working with these brands was that they genuinely supported netball and pumped money into advertising the sport so that it could get the recognition it deserves. I loved the passion in every campaign we set out to do. It was a bonus to me that each deal steadily topped up my bank account, but the commitments were intense. Whether I was shooting advertisements, doing photoshoots or running workshops, I soon discovered that there was a lot more involved with ambassador work than just letting companies use your image.

Unlike my male counterparts, I had to do a lot more work to earn coin. As a female athlete, we earn less for an ambassador role than our male counterparts because the brand isn't as 'valuable'. There's not as much reach due to less marketing and coverage on TV, so we aren't valued as highly. Despite being one of the top twelve in a sport that millions around the country play, as opposed to being one of the top four hundred (as in AFL), these footballers got more for one photoshoot than I got for a twelve-month deal. However, I wasn't in a position to complain because I was still earning more than most who were playing netball.

It was great to have extra money coming in and I knew I needed to save for the future because I'd be starting from zero when I finally retired. You go from being one of the best in the world at something, to the bottom in whatever you decide to do for a career afterwards, which is terrifyingly confronting for someone who has been at the top. Once the sponsors started rolling in, I was grateful to be recognised for all of the hard work I'd put into my brand for over a decade now, and felt lucky to be working with such great companies. I wanted to make sure that I was giving back to these brands that were making my life easier. I also knew that new athletes are always waiting around the corner, so I was happy to soak up my time in the sun.

Times you should apologise #63

When you scream at your tandem parachute guy not to jump off the 'fucking cliff' because you have deadset changed your mind, but he does anyway and it ends up being a life changing experience.

(SORRY FOR BEING A DRAMA QUEEN, PARACHUTE MAN)

CHAPTER TWENTY-ONE

ARE YOU WITH ME?

At the start of 2015, the Swifts recruited a cracking Goal Defender, Julie Corletto, and she played a big part in me improving my game that year. Julie taught me about video analysis, and how to pick my game apart by watching myself. She also showed me how to watch the opposition play and work out how to pick them apart as a partnership. I'd be chilling at home mid-week and suddenly receive thirty videos with accompanying text on what we'd need to do to beat them.

There is so much that goes on behind the scenes in making a great athlete; 90 per cent of the work gets done before you even step out on court on game day, the last 10 per cent is putting together everything you have prepared for physically and mentally.

As an athlete, if you have a bad performance, your instinct is to ask yourself why. Did you do your prep? Did you take the time to figure out if you prepared for a game properly? Did you get a good night's sleep? Eat the right food? Watch videos to analyse your opposition? Physically train for what you needed to do against them? Chat to your teammates about the role they need to play in helping you? Did you ask how you could help them? Did you do your strength and conditioning program to keep you strong and fast? Did you have physio to make sure you didn't have any niggles on game day? Did you see your sports psychologist to discuss the poor, or good, performance you had the week before?

As you can see, there is a lot that goes into being an elite athlete – and even more that goes into being a great one. Most female athletes need to balance all of this work with another job as well.

Fortunately at this point in my career, I had the time to recover well as I didn't have to work outside of playing, so I was physically strong and highly skilled. The extra footwork sessions with Rob were helping to hone my skills to make sure I could move my feet more quickly than any other Goal Keeper in the competition. I loved Rob's attitude to training and the brand he was teaching. Defenders need speedy footwork to get around attackers. In netball, you can't touch players on the other team at all while the ball is in their hands, so it's important to be able to move your feet and change your body angle as fast as possible to get the ball off your opponent.

He also made it so fun. He would hold a big blue crash pad and stand between me and a ball. The game? I had to use quick footwork to get the ball without letting him whack me with this giant crash pad. It was hilarious. He called the game 'Keep the Blue Off You'. This is just a snippet of why I enjoyed having Rob as a coach so much because he made netball so enjoyable and came up with new and different training techniques.

For non-netty-heads out there, quick footwork is necessary to confuse the thrower. If I hedged up towards a player, I knew the players on the centre court would try and throw to the shooter behind me. When I could change direction *fast,* I was able to jump and intercept the ball before they caught it. Alternatively, if I covered my shooter well enough, I knew the other team would throw to their teammate on the edge of the circle, and I could move quickly to intercept that ball, too. A Goal Keeper is restricted to the goal third of the court, which is about 150 square metres. It's an area that isn't too difficult to cover, if you move quickly enough. I learned to do this incredibly well and prided myself on it.

By the first game of the 2015 season, I was ready to back myself physically and mentally. I started out playing great, consistent netball and Rob was happy with the way I was training and playing. I knew my performance was due in a large part to the people around me, and the positive vibes I was receiving from Rob and Julie. Also, my teammates were selfless athletes who got the best out of others and complemented my game, too.

Most athletes I've met over the years were not only committed to their own success, but also to the success of those on their team. The Swifts girls were great examples of this. They were professional in every sense, including their diet, their training and the enjoyment they got from life without taking netball too seriously. Everything I learned from these girls contributed to me playing the best I could. I loved being on court with them and it was showing in my game.

I was averaging six intercepts per match, which is considered a lot in professional netball, and I had a personal goal to reach ten. No-one I played against was going to have an easy game. My opponents usually feared me because I played the mental game.

My prime motivation in any game is to win. For me, this meant I needed to be the dominant player and I was determined to make my opponent's life a living hell for the full sixty minutes on court. I wanted my opponent to know that, from the moment I walked onto the court for warm-up, I was watching everything she was doing. A lot of team sport is about mind games, so I'd try my hardest to get inside my opponent's head. One of the ways I did this was by trying to restrict their space, which would confuse the player throwing the ball to them.

The Shooter/Keeper dynamic is like a game of chess. We're constantly watching each other, trying to get in the best position and be in the best spot to get, or spoil, the ball. Having a little bit of mongrel in me helps too. There's an old saying in netball that the defenders are the mongrels, and the shooters are the princesses. I figured that if the shooters were thinking about me and not the ball, I'd already half won the battle.

I've always been loud. Goal Keepers have always been known to yell instructions to their team, but I was blessed with a loud, deep voice that not only instructed my teammates, but also annoyed the opposition. I'd always been vocal during netball games but had never really thought much about it. Staying engaged and being loud gave me the energy to keep going without dropping my head. I may not have been the best player, but I would never give up and that encouraged my teammates to never give up either. It also gave me the ability to get on top of my opponents because if they started beating me, I would find a new way to overcome them.

Over the years I had added a lot of tools to my toolkit and prided myself on being able to play tall players, short players and fast players. I loved being versatile. I also loved it when they started sledging me or talking smack because it meant I was getting under their skin and doing a good job! In every netball team I'd ever played in, I was the one who'd roar down the court at my teammates to spur them on and get our team spirit and adrenaline pumping. But this was my first time playing on the main stage and my loudmouth behaviour was suddenly starting to get attention from the public.

As far as I was concerned it was a win-win. I loved getting up and about, which would get the crowd up and about. And when the crowd was energised, I would feed off their energy and play even better. I felt like I had a connection with the fans, and they seemed to get a kick out of the way I was playing. Our supporter base was also the supporter base for Western Sydney Wanderers Soccer Team. They were loud and would make up songs for the game. They started '*You are my Sharni, my only Sharni, you make me happy when times are grey. You'll never know dear, how much we love you, so please don't take our Sharni away.*' Like, isn't that the best?! Even young boys and their dads were coming to watch me play, and this was a demographic our sport had always struggled with. Our main demographic had always been ten-to-fourteen-year-old girls, but now I had women coming up and asking if they could have photos for their boyfriends, sons and husbands!

I was having an impact and I could feel it. It was my second year playing for the Swifts and the people in the crowd were big Sharni fans. The feeling was mutual. I LOVED playing in front of them. They spurred me on, and thanks to them, I played even better. I had always been a high-energy athlete, and the more the crowd screamed, the more eccentric I became. There was a 'Who's your favourite player?' initiative and I had 80 per cent of the votes. But it was the love I felt from the crowd that blew my mind in every game, even when we played in New Zealand.

'You are the only player I've ever heard to get the loudest cheer even when you're playing in the away team!' Rob said to me.

I was so grateful to the fans for supporting me, and us as a team. They were the reason I was being paid properly. If they didn't pay to come to our games, buy our merch or turn on their TVs to watch the games, I would not be a professional female athlete. And I wanted to show them how grateful I was. Before each game I would wave and blow kisses to them as a way of saying thank you for being here, and I'd stay back and sign autographs for anyone who wanted them after the match. Sometimes my team manager would almost have to drag me away by the ear, and my teammates would be annoyed because we couldn't do our post-match chat until I was there.

'Hurry up, Sharni!' they'd shout.

But I didn't care. If it wasn't for the people supporting us, we wouldn't be there and I refused to say no to someone. Even if my team manager was dragging me away, I'd be reaching out to high-five every kid that missed out on a signature.

The interaction and love affair I had with the fans made me popular, but it wasn't the only reason I was starting to become well-known. After doing radio in Adelaide, I'd made the move to TV soon after arriving in the big smoke. Turns out being a loudmouth mongrel Goal Keeper was a bonus in the media!

Rebecca Trbojevich, the media chick for the Swifts, got me in and on EVERYTHING. I was so grateful to her then, and now, for helping me get my media career up and running. I appeared on a TV show called *SportsFan Clubhouse*, which had over a hundred thousand viewers weekly, as well as Channel 9's *Wide World of Sport* every couple of weeks. These shows were a great platform to showcase my knowledge of sport and human behaviour, and gave me the chance to comment on all sports outside netball.

Never shy to share my opinion on anything, I would get some viewers offside, but I got a lot of people onside, too. I grabbed these media opportunities with both hands and made the most of them. Also, like I've said, the World Cup coming to Sydney was a huge deal. Only held once every four years, it is netball's Olympics and I wanted our sport to be everywhere. I threw my hand up for every appearance, some paid but most not.

A lot of the netball players aren't really into these appearances, but I saw them as the perfect opportunity for building our brand. Also, the connections, networks and growing fanbase was so valuable to our sport, and I knew it would set me up with another career path in the future.

My netball was still improving, which was in large part due to the positive environment I was in. I loved my teammates and my coach. We made the Grand Final that year, against the Queensland Firebirds, which was an unforgettable game. We were up the whole game, and then Gretel Tippett scored the winning goal with only ten seconds left and we lost by one. It was heartbreaking. I was MVP but in a losing team, so it meant nothing to me. I wanted the gold for all of the hard work we had done. We knew Julie Corletto (nee Prendergast) was retiring at the end of the year and it killed me that we couldn't get her the win to finish off her phenomenal career.

Jules had taught me so much about professionalism and was a big part of why my game went to the next level. She taught me how to be more present during the game, and if something wasn't working, we'd change it straight away. We were in sync and knew exactly what we had to do to get the ball. She'd set me up for intercept after intercept and I wouldn't have been able to take any of the glory without her by my side. Jules never wanted glory. She was just happy going about her business. As long as we got the win, that was all that mattered. This is what made that Grand Final loss so hard to swallow.

Here is this final match that you've put all your time and energy into getting to for twelve months and you're willing to give up everything to get there and win it. You don't see your family or friends, you miss weddings and birthdays, sometimes even funerals. (I didn't get to say goodbye to my grandpa because I was in New Zealand playing netball and I know a lot of the girls have had similar experiences.) I gave up on a career outside of netball to make this sport my life. I wasn't fully invested in any relationship I had during this time, because no man was going to be more important than my netball career. I had all of my eggs in one basket and that basket was netball. If we hadn't made the Grand Final, it would have been easier to deal with because we were never in it.

Losing a Grand Final like that feels almost like having a huge crush on someone to the point where you think you're in love, and after a year they ask you out on a date. You can't believe it. *Yay!* You are going on a first date with the love of your life and you'll probably even get married. But then you go on the date and you fall at the last hurdle. A question is asked, it doesn't work out and they tell you they never want to see you again. It's over and it breaks your heart. That's what losing a Grand Final feels like when you're ending your career. For those who continue to play, don't stress. There's still a chance with that hot crush next year.

I was relieved when I was selected for the 2015 World Cup team. Although I was feeling confident, I knew better than to take selection for granted. You just knew there was someone creeping up behind you to be the next best thing. Although I'd been picked for the Commonwealth Games the year before, I wasn't secure in my spot and knew not to take anything as a given.

I became somewhat of a poster girl, having played with the Swifts and with the World Cup being played on home soil, and was being pulled left, right and centre for publicity. While our domestic competition has always struggled against the likes of the AFL and NRL, when we netballers play for Australia, everyone gets behind us.

Every one of our games had more than 12,000 spectators, and all of our Finals were played to a sold-out stadium of 17,500 people. It was unreal and the noise was electric. The love I got from the crowd blew my mind every game. It was a level up from what I got when playing in the Swifts games. I always struggled a bit more in the Diamonds environment than that of the Swifts, though. The Swifts loved that I engaged the crowd, and I was allowed to be myself, whereas once the World Cup had started, I was getting in trouble from the coach for waving to the crowd because they went too crazy. But it wasn't distracting me, it was actually helping me get my energy up for the game. When I wasn't allowed to interact with the crowd in the way I would have liked, I felt that my personality was being quashed, and then I didn't have the same 'oomph' when I played for the Diamonds. Even though I'd learned not to let things like this bring me down, it still takes its toll. And because I appreciate the crowd, I continued to wave anyway. There's nothing like getting the fans fired up! As I continued to wave, I just made it sneakier. Gotta give the people what they want. No apologies there.

I had never been considered a starting player for Australia, but this tournament was different for me. The only problem was that I was a strong Goal Keeper and the coach wanted me to play Goal Defence, due to our Captain, Laura Geitz, also being a top Goal Keeper. Julie Corletto was by far the best Goal Defence in the world and deserved that spot. Still, I felt honoured to be starting in my second-ever game against New Zealand after five years of representing Australia (I had started in other games, but not against New Zealand – this is the goal for any Australian netballer). But I didn't play my best and subsequently got dragged. Julie came on and did a fantastic job, but the Diamonds ended up losing the game. I was kicking myself afterwards, especially because it brought back so many bad memories of not feeling good enough.

But we had a game the next day, so I had to get over it pretty quickly. It was a frustrating tournament all up. Poor Jules was injured throughout the whole thing, which meant she had to spend training days resting. This meant that the defenders had to do double the training load, as you can't sub-out and rest when you have one less rotation. I was struggling with the workload and felt like I was cooked come game time.

I was absolutely exhausted, but I was still trying to push my case to be put back in Goal Keeper. I knew that this was probably not going to be possible, but I held on to hope and wouldn't stop fighting for it until the tournament was over. That didn't mean I had anything against Geitzy, our Captain. She was, and still is, a very good friend of mine. Wanting to take her position had nothing to do with her personally and she knew that. We all fought to play, but never took the result out on each other. We always supported each other and gave each other feedback in an effort to improve ourselves. It was women empowering women, not tearing each other down. 'Sisters in arms' is our motto and we lived by it.

From then on it was tough to get back on the court. The crowd would cheer my name and yell '*HOO, HA*' when I stepped on the court, and they rode every part of the emotional roller-coaster with me. And I bloody loved it. I felt them, and I knew they felt me, too.

By the time the Semi-Final against Jamaica came along I was itching to get out on that court. I didn't start the game, nor did I come on at half-time. I sat on the bench, fidgeting and praying that I would get a chance to go on. By this stage I knew I wouldn't be playing in the Grand Final, because if you're not starting in the Semi, you're certainly not starting in the Final unless there's a serious injury. So, I sat and waited.

The game was approaching the end of the third quarter when I saw my coach nod at me. This was the sign to start warming up because she was going to put me on. We were leading by enough goals that it wasn't a risk to put me on. I got up and started jogging in the corner of the court. A few seconds later the whole crowd – all 17,500 of them – started a chant.

'Sharni! Sharni!'

Even though the game was still going on in front of me.

The break came and I bibbed up. For me, that fourth quarter was my Grand Final. I had a cracker and the crowd loved it. I wanted to play well for them, for our country and for all the support they had given me. Not only in the moment, but also over my whole career. I couldn't have done it without them. We won the game and went on to play in the Grand Final.

As expected, I didn't get a guernsey on that day. But as much as I wanted it, I was content to sit on the bench because I knew there was nothing more I could have done. At the end of the day, we were doing it for Australia. Not ourselves.

We started out with a wicked lead and although they crept back, it wasn't enough to deny us the win. We had played eight games in ten days and despite being physically and emotionally buggered *we won*! It had been a long time since any country had claimed Commonwealth Games/World Cup back-to-back wins and we were ecstatic.

We signed autographs and paraded around the court like the champions we were. After receiving our medals, we popped champagne in the change rooms and sang our favourite songs at the top of our voices. We played 'Are You With Me', as we had before each game, and it's still my ringtone to this day because of the joy that tournament brought me. As usual, my deep baritone could be heard above all the other (much higher) singing voices! Back to the hotel for a quick shower before heading to the post-tournament function at the Museum of Contemporary Art in Sydney where we rocked the night away.

The best part about the party after a win is celebrating with all the people who helped you on the journey. The support staff and

Netball Australia staff, your families and all of the past players who the win means just as much to. Caitlin Bassett and I were being loud and rowdy, as per usual. There was a moment when we just clinked our glasses together and laughed.

'One of us will probably be the next Australian Captain, isn't that insane?!' Caitlin said.

We were the young ones in the team but I had been a part of the Diamonds since 2011, and Caitlin had been since 2008. We knew Laura and a few of the other girls would retire in the coming years (and they did soon after that World Cup) which meant there would be a lot of new girls on the team. With our years of experience we hoped we'd be the most likely contenders for captaincy.

My time with the Swifts was the springboard I needed to reach new heights in netball. Heights I never *dared* dream about. But it was also the start of a pattern that would be my eventual undoing.

Times you should apologise #21

When you're at the World Cup after party and you squat underneath your High Performance Manager's legs and stand up with him on your shoulders, then keep dancing with him up there and refuse to put him down even though he's scared for his life.
(SORRY, ANDREW)

CHAPTER TWENTY-TWO

SHARNI THE NETBALLER

Nic and I finally broke up after the 2015 World Cup. I knew this was an inevitability before the Cup began, but when you are about to play in one of the biggest events in netball, you're advised by the Australian team to avoid making huge life changes because you don't want any added emotional stressors, or to take your eye off the prize.

I had actually tried breaking up with Nic the summer before, but he was a stubborn guy and wouldn't leave. Hurting someone else sucks, so after that first break-up fail, I'd continued to avoid the reality of the situation. When you've been living in denial for so long and finally find the courage to pull the trigger, only to have him say, 'Nope, I'm not leaving,' it's a kick in the guts. I didn't know what to do. So, I let him stay but we both knew the relationship was over. I couldn't deal with the emotional turmoil of breaking his heart, so I parked my feelings and focused on my netball, which thankfully kept me busy all year round. But once the World Cup was over, I tried again. This time he got the message and agreed we needed to end it. I had already planned my escape after having 'the talk', organising a solo holiday to Byron Bay. This would give Nic the time and space he needed to move out while I was gone. It would also give me time to be alone, reset and reassess my goals.

I hired a glamping hut with no access to wi-fi in the Hinterland Regional Park for five days, hired a car and drove out there with Deepak Chopra's *The Seven Spiritual Laws of Success* in my bag. While there, I had a pretty chilled-out and idyllic routine. I'd wake up, do yoga, go for a hike, then come back to the hut, read a chapter and journal my thoughts for hours on end. It was a great healing experience, and allowed me to hit the reset button after what had been a hectic few years.

One excerpt from my journal from that time reads:

8 December 2015

I have always had a fear of success. I've always wanted to do well but have feared the success that comes with it. Not anymore, as I now understand insecurities within myself and I know that by being true to myself I am not underneath anybody, nor am I above anybody ... It is awesome to be able to see my flaws so clearly and to feel them in my gut. To know that they are there, but that I can now do something about it to create more love, joy and abundance in my life.

I'm excited to take a stand today and make a real shift in my life. To apply what I have learned into daily rituals. As my life coach, Dave, would say, 'Start to build the piggybank of self-trust and self-love, as this is where confidence comes from.'

Even when it comes to relationships, I always have a fear around something. A fear of staying in it, a fear of getting out of it. Fear of hurting someone's feelings. Fear of not being enough. Reflecting now, it all seems so silly. If you are happy being you, just BE YOU.

This was day one! As you can imagine, I went deep into unpacking what my ego wanted and replacing it with the needs of my true self.

Before this little spiritual getaway, I'd started doing work to try and understand myself and what was important to me in life. I had a life coach for when things got a bit fuzzy, but I was always trying to keep myself on track. Unfortunately, I soon found that it was a lot harder to be myself in the netball environment than I had hoped. The more I let my guard down to come from a place of love, the more I was criticised for being who I was, and this, in turn, had a detrimental effect on my mental health.

But I came back from that solitary trip with a better sense of self than I'd ever had before. It's funny, though, because now when I reflect, I was still doing personal development to be a better netballer, not a better person, which was also a contributor to my undoing. My netball career was continuing on an upward swing, and my popularity with the crowds and the public didn't seem to be waning. I was on top of the world as far as my career and profile were concerned, and for the first time in my life I didn't have to worry about money, which was a huge relief. I was on *SportsFan Clubhouse*, Fox Sports, Nine's *Wide World of Sports* and doing regular radio spots on multiple stations. If there was an event on, I was there. But despite being one of the highest-paid netballers, I was still on the same wage as a first-year AFL player. This was what motivated me to continue to get my sport in the headlines, so we could get more sponsorships and better broadcast deals, then I could push for our players to be paid what we were worth. The time and effort we put in was exceptional, our professionalism was next level, and there was nothing left that we could do on the court to make our game any better. The sport was at its peak and now we just needed the wider world to notice us.

I decided to hire my own personal trainer. The personal trainer for the Swifts had twelve athletes to look after, and I figured that if I had my own, I could get better results with the individual attention. I knew that the awesome New Zealand player Irene van Dyk had done the same thing, and it had improved her fitness and game so much that she'd played until she was forty-two. *Maybe I can do that, too*, I thought. My trainer, Lachlan McKinnon, was amazing. He knew my body and was able to get the most out of me. My game went through the roof once I started working with him, thanks to the added strength I gained. Rob Wright and the team were totally supportive of me working with Lachlan, especially since I was playing better for it, but Netball Australia wasn't happy about me hiring my own trainer.

They organised a meeting between me and six of their people, and asked me, 'Do you think you're an NBA player?' and, 'Who do you think you are?'

I didn't understand why it would be a bad thing if I wanted to bring the sport up to where the NBA was. The NBA is one of the biggest sporting leagues in the world, so I didn't see a problem in wanting to emulate those athletes to get the most out of myself. Little did they know, I was actually modelling myself on a New Zealand netballer.

I knew they would have an issue with it, so I had it written into my contract that I could have my own trainer, in which case the Diamonds had no legal grounds to stop me training with someone else. I stood my ground and kept the emotion out of it.

'No, I just want to be the best netballer I can be,' I said. 'And I don't understand why there's an issue with that.'

By the end of the meeting, they hadn't managed to persuade me to give Lachlan up, but I was annoyed at their attempt to bully me into doing something they wanted. I felt like I had been ganged up on, with six of them and one of me in the room, and I hadn't been given the opportunity to have a representative there with me. I actually thought that was extremely poor management by them.

It was 2016, my third year with the Swifts. I was playing well, was in peak physical condition, and was loving my teammates and coach. I was so busy and single-minded that I didn't notice that my sporting career had taken over all aspects of my life. I was on a dangerous road of 'achieve, achieve, achieve' and was pushing myself to be better and better every time I stepped on the netball court. If I got nine intercepts in a game, I'd beat myself up because it wasn't ten. Unfortunately, the most dangerous person you can compete against is the avatar of yourself you create in your mind. That avatar will *always* be better than you, and it's a vicious downward spiral from then on. A 'What now?' spiral. And that was the direction I was well and truly heading in.

I had the best international tour of my career in England, getting MVP in all three matches and MVP of the whole tournament. Not only was I popular in Australia and New Zealand, but I also now had a 'Sharni Army' fanbase in England, too. The crowd there was wild and cheered for me, even though

I was playing for the other team. I loved it. I took the confidence boost I got from this experience into the Swifts season and had another blinder of a year. With the help of Rob Wright, Lachlan and my psychologist, Jenny, I'd built myself into a stand-out player and was finally receiving the recognition from the public that I'd always wanted. But I was also learning that this kind of attention wasn't anywhere near as fulfilling as being with people who really knew and loved me, and as I started reaching my goals, one after another, I just felt emptier and emptier. I was doing the work, but it felt like something was missing and I couldn't put my finger on what it was that was making me feel sad all the time.

Since Nic and I had broken up I'd been living by myself with two cats I rescued from the RSPCA, Chiggy and Xena. It was lonely, and I started missing my family and friends. When Kara gave birth to her first child, Aaliyah, I was playing in Sydney and couldn't be there. I flew down during the week to meet my first niece, but the brief visit only reinforced a nagging feeling that I was missing out on something that life was truly about. I'd always loved going home to see my family, but this time I felt envious of how simple and uncomplicated their lives were. It hurt knowing I wouldn't be with my new baby niece and, after being away from my family for nine years, I couldn't shake the feeling that I wasn't where I needed to be. Aaliyah's birth was the beginning of a crushing sadness and loneliness that began to slowly envelop me. Human connection has always been important to me, and I began to see I didn't have nearly enough of that in Sydney.

When I was living in Adelaide, I was always out and about, meeting friends when I wasn't training or playing, and had close non-netball mates. I could be 'Sharni the human' with them, not just 'Sharni the netballer', but I started to lose this balance when I moved to Sydney. I still went adventuring and hiking in the great outdoors when I could, but I was so busy playing netball and building my brand that I rarely had any time to chill out and be with non-sporty people and animals the way I always had been. I was constantly around lots of people, but they were all connected to netball. I wasn't having conversations about other things I cared about, like horses or travel or spirituality. Katie was living in Sydney at the time, too, but our music industry and netball industry calendars clashed, and we rarely found time to catch up. I had a good group of teammates, but you couldn't have a conversation without the subject of netball coming up.

The recurring, non-serving self-belief that I wasn't enough kept popping up again and again, too. The year before, Laura Geitz (Captain) and Renae Ingles took a break from the 2015 international tour after playing nonstop for years on end. This should have been an opportunity for some of us in the team to step up but when we lost a game in Melbourne by three goals, the Diamonds coach panicked. She brought Laura back from her holiday in New Zealand, and Renae back from a calf strain, to play the last game of the tour in Perth, which meant dropping two players from the team. I was pushed back out to Goal Defence, a position I didn't play, and the rest of the team was shattered, too. We had nothing against Laura or Renae, of course, but knowing the coach didn't trust us to do the job without them stung. It shattered our confidence and, as a result, we went on to lose by eleven goals, even with Renae and Laura.

This is where I believe the Australian team started to slide, as this experience affected our confidence and we didn't hit the mark at the next Commonwealth Games or the World Cup. At the time I couldn't see how much it had affected my confidence personally. I felt like I deserved to play, but I didn't challenge the situation when I should have, and I take responsibility for that. Netball isn't an environment where players are encouraged to challenge the coach. We are taught to respect and obey, and we do it well. And I was always being called out for my strong-mindedness and for challenging the status quo.

At the end of that tour, I was hounded again by the Australian coach and the Diamonds' strength and conditioning coach who wanted me to follow their strength and conditioning program, even though I knew my own program was working much better for me as an individual.

I tried to explain why the program I was doing was more helpful to me but they wouldn't listen and told me I was doing the wrong thing. When I started to cry, they told me I needed to toughen up.

'You need to harden up, Sharni, and learn how to grind things out.'

I may have been crying but I wasn't backing down.

'You know what, guys? If you tell me to grind it out, I'm going to end up hating netball and quit,' I said, then got up and walked out. I can see the irony now, reflecting on this time: it was the end of the tour but the start of my crash.

The crash happens because you've pushed yourself so hard all year and by the time you've played that last game, you have no energy left to give to anyone or anything else. The three years I spent in Sydney were all '*werk, werk, werk*'. And when you work that hard for weeks and months at a time, it eventually takes a toll.

For three years in a row, I had trained and played with the Swifts for six months of the year, then gone straight into Australian team commitments for five months. I'd be completely burnt out by the end of the international season. It was a never-ending cycle, and when I was in the eye of the storm there wasn't time to stop and think.

But that meeting with the Diamonds coaches destroyed me. I went home and climbed into bed and pretty much stayed there until the Swifts preseason started three weeks later.

Athletes tend to be perfectionists and are harder on themselves than anyone else. I didn't understand why they couldn't see I was just trying to be the best I could be – yes, for me, but also for the team. I wanted to take netball to new heights, and I couldn't do that if I did what everybody else did. If I did that, then the sport would stay the same. But the constant judgement of my character was wearing me down. In those three weeks in bed, I decided to keep my head down and let my actions on the court speak louder than words. I knew my Swifts coach and teammates loved and accepted me for who I was, and that was all that mattered.

I'd been good at keeping up with my regular therapy sessions when I first arrived in Sydney, but by the third year I had let it slip and was going months without a session. I was losing my sense of self. I was Sharni the netballer – but who else was I? I started to feel empty all the time. I was lost and lonely, even when I was with other people. It felt like I was mainly surrounded by people who wanted something from me, rather than just wanting to be with me, for my company. Of course, I had people in my life who weren't like this, but I wasn't spending enough time with them.

When I won the 2016 Australian Netballer for the ANZ

Championship, and International Netballer of the Year, I was stoked. But when the awards night was cancelled for reasons unknown, those happy feelings instantly vanished. It wasn't enough that I had won; I was aiming for the Liz Ellis Diamond, which I would have been a contender for, but due to not having an awards night it wasn't awarded in 2016. Having the other two awards separately still wasn't enough. Nothing was ever enough.

By the end of 2016 I had two premierships, a Commonwealth Games gold medal and two World Championship gold medals under my belt, and the Australian team had never lost a tour that I'd been a part of. But inside, I was empty. A catalyst for me was after the 2016 ANZ Championship season, when I had a leadership camp in Melbourne and was staying in the city. Because I had to fly in and out for commitments in Sydney, even though I was in Melbourne I couldn't see my family. That night I called them from my hotel room, and I was hysterical.

'I'm so lonely,' I sobbed to them over the phone. I remember Mum, my sister Kara and my uncle Graeme talking to me, trying to calm me down and just wanting to support me.

'I'm surrounded by people all day every day, but I'm just so lonely.'

I didn't know what was going on, but it made me realise I had to come home to my support networks. And the timing was right; Netball Australia was breaking up with Netball New Zealand due to a new broadcast deal with Channel 9, so the ANZ Championship was coming to an end, and Super Netball was about to be born. Kara was pregnant with her second child, so when I heard whispers that my favourite football team, Collingwood, were creating a new netball team, I sat down to write a pros and cons list for going back to Melbourne. My new housemate and Adelaide brother, Dan, had moved to Sydney halfway through 2016 to work as a lawyer and was there to help me with my list and the decision-making process. There were a lot of pros to staying in Sydney, but the thing that outweighed everything else, including ongoing success in my career, was my family. I bit the bullet and started planning to move back home to Melbourne.

Times you should apologise #143

When you buy a new bed and it's delivered while you're away on tour so your housemate has to move the old bed out and hurts his back.
(SORRY, DAN)

CHAPTER TWENTY-THREE

TUCK IN YOUR SHIRT

I moved back to Melbourne in October 2016. My old Kestrels mate Mel Kitchin was moving back, too, so we found a house together in South Melbourne. Being the hipsters we were, we christened it the 'PuPaSoMe' (Pussy Palace of South Melbourne) because I now owned three cats. Mel and I hadn't lived in the same state since 2012, but it felt as if we hadn't been apart for a single day.

I'd hoped that moving back to my home city of Melbourne would cure the empty, sad feelings I'd started having in Sydney, but unfortunately it wasn't going to be that simple. Whatever was starting to happen in my brain went deeper than I realised at the time, and it would be a while before I worked out that there was more going on than I could have imagined.

I had another tour with the Australian team before starting the season with my new Collingwood team, and in the lead-up to the tournament I received a call from the Australian coach.

'Sharni, come meet me next week for a coffee.'

I was slightly apprehensive as I headed off to our meeting. The coach knew about my move back to Melbourne and had been supportive, but our relationship was still slightly rocky. We had known each other for a long time and respected one another, but there was a lack of trust and openness between us.

'Caitlin Bassett isn't coming on the next tour,' she told me, 'so I've decided to make you Captain of the upcoming Quad Series to South Africa and England.'

These were the words I'd been waiting to hear my whole career, which is why what came out of my mouth was a surprise to me … and her.

'Are you sure?'

'Yes, I'm sure, Sharni.'

I thanked her, and said how grateful I was for the opportunity, but couldn't shake the feeling that I hadn't earned and didn't deserve the position. I wasn't sure I was Aussie Captain material. I was outspoken and often got in trouble for not being overly professional in media interviews. It wasn't unusual for me to unintentionally ruffle feathers, just by being myself, and the previous Aussie captains had all been very different to me. They were similar in their professional approaches to the media, always saying the right thing and acting in an appropriate manner, and in how they portrayed themselves in a 'proper' way. I was loud and rough and loved making people laugh, which often meant saying exactly what was on my mind, instead of what I 'should' say. But with Caitlin resting, I was also the most experienced Diamond going on tour, so I guessed it made sense. These were the thoughts racing through my mind as I sat across from the Diamonds coach that day.

I think that even then I knew I'd never be the kind of Australian netball captain anyone wanted me to be, not anyone within the team or organisation anyway. Being myself had only ever gotten me in trouble and rubbed people the wrong way. And now I was expected to lead my team? And how would the team take the news? It was usually a position voted by the team, but this had been handed to me by the coach.

I was scared shitless and didn't know if I wanted the kind of pressure that went along with being Captain of the Aussie team, but all I could do was be my best, play my best, and well, hope for the best.

My teammates congratulated me on my new role as Captain and we all headed off for the Quad Series. We got off to a great start, winning three out of three games against New Zealand, South Africa and England, but the whole time we were away and playing, I never once felt like a Captain. There was more of a leadership group vibe happening, and I was lucky to have the support of Caitlin Thwaites and Kim Ravaillion, but the role didn't feel right to me. I wasn't in the right headspace to make decisions whenever I had the chance, so our team usually ended up doing what the coach wanted us to do and was led by her. This, of course, made me feel like a failure, even though I was playing well, and we were winning all our games. I came home from that tour feeling like I'd completely wasted, and failed at, the important once-in-a-lifetime role I'd been given.

Back in Melbourne, there was no break, as I went straight into training with the Collingwood team. It was a challenge from the get-go, as there was no previous culture for us as a team to mould ourselves into. We tried building it ourselves but were given no real direction.

During preseason, we were made to do a team-bonding

activity that involved each of us sharing our darkest secrets. All the girls started crying, so I cried, too, but only because everyone else was. I actually felt nothing, which made me feel terrible. Did I just not care about these girls' issues and problems? Was I becoming a monster? This was a bonding session and I was having trouble connecting with anyone there, except my mate, Ash Braz. Sitting there listening to everyone, all I could think was, *Why are we sharing such personal information with each other when we're here to play netball?* I was a process-driven athlete and I just wanted to play.

Please know that a lot of these realisations are a lot easier upon reflection. During this time all I felt was the unease and uncertainty. I didn't know why I was feeling the way that I was but now that I've had the opportunity to put all my thoughts down and have done the psychological work, I understand why I was feeling this way and can articulate it. The experience I'd had of personal issues getting mixed up with netball in Adelaide had turned out to be a disaster. I just couldn't understand why everyone needed to be involved in everyone else's business when it had nothing to do with them. The session was an awkward start and I found the whole situation pretty upsetting.

What the fuck have I got myself into? I thought.

There were five of us who had played for the Diamonds in the Quad Series who had come back to Melbourne to play for Collingwood, and the pressure was on us to perform in our new team. With such experienced players, it felt as though the coach automatically assumed we'd win every game, and we, too, expected to do well, but, unfortunately, expectations don't always create positive results.

We lost our first game to the Melbourne Vixens by three goals and there was a new rivalry born between two Melbourne clubs. Although it wasn't the result we were after, it still wasn't the worst result either. We were a brand-new team, and we had worked our arses off in that preseason, so losing that game saw the start of a negative team culture.

We were all so hard on ourselves, and the coaching staff were, too. If I could turn back time, I would have loved to have been in a positive frame of mind to remind us all how well we were going. But we were all being crushed by the weight of the expectations the whole netball world had placed on us, which wasn't even as heavy as the weight of those we had placed on ourselves and each other.

This whole chapter in my life is a bit of a blur because of the emotional turmoil I was feeling. We were playing okay, but not great. We were winning some games, but we weren't performing as expected. As each game went on, the negativity from the coaching staff and therefore us got worse and worse, triggering poorer and poorer performances. I still wasn't in the right frame of mind either. I didn't know why I couldn't draw from all of my experience and have a positive impact on the team. The frustration with myself was real and, unfortunately, that then reflected on my teammates, too. I was becoming snappy at training, and that wasn't me either – I had always been so positive. I didn't know why I was being so blunt, but because I didn't have much of a filter, I ended up getting a few of my teammates offside. I now know that the reason I wasn't being myself was that I had depression, and that this irritability was a common symptom. I didn't know this at the time, so I just became angrier and angrier with myself and the situation.

We were all friends in the team, and it was nice that we cared about each other off the court. Despite me not connecting to the teary bonding sessions, it was incredibly courageous of the players to share the stories they did. But I felt this had a detrimental impact on our performance. It meant we were too worried about each other to have tough conversations. Some of my teammates thought I just didn't care, simply because I was blunt, and my tone could be sharp, but caring to me means having tough conversations. To other players, though, caring meant not saying some things that they felt needed to be said because they didn't want to hurt another player's feelings. I found the environment increasingly frustrating because little issues weren't being addressed, and so they became problems. I believe having tough conversations means you can talk out what's going on and find a solution for the issue. But once again, this all sounds great upon reflection. At the time I was just frustrated and angry.

Throughout my netball career I'd been known as the girl with the booming voice on the court. But after things weren't going our way halfway through the season, and we were trying to find reasons why, it was suggested that I needed to change the tone of my voice on the court. I was told that it wasn't the proper way to behave and that it was bugging girls during the game, but I didn't understand why this was the case when this is was how I had played my *whole* career. Instead of the progressive environment I had been in with the New South Wales Swifts, it felt more like the Diamonds environment where people weren't comfortable with me being myself, which in turn meant that my netball performance started to decline. I wasn't playing horrifically, but I wasn't playing as well as I was the year before either.

When I was playing netball as a kid, there was always one club member, usually an older woman, who'd yell over the loudspeaker, 'Can the girls on Court Two please tuck their shirts in?' I was generally the girl with her shirt untucked. Netball is a 'proper' sport, and appearance is important, but I could never understand it (and still don't) because tucking my shirt in had no impact on how well I played. As much as the sport is moving forwards, I feel that netball still very much has a 'do what you're told and don't question it' culture. And I have never been someone who responded well to this kind of philosophy.

It wasn't just me that the blame fell on. Disappointingly, our younger players copped it, too. When mature players in the team don't take responsibility for their performances and blame the younger players, it's never going to go down well. I am also very sad that I couldn't do something about this; I think I was in self-protect mode, but it pains me to this day that it may have affected these players' confidence and careers. It was totally unfair. If you want to be a good athlete, reflect on your own performance and don't blame anybody else. Great athletes take responsibility for their actions; they don't try to find a situation or person to blame.

My despondent mood also had a lot to do with the fact I never had time to see my family or friends – the main reason I'd come back to Melbourne. I started worrying that the move had been a mistake, but there was nothing I could do about it now. It was my decision and I had to live with it. The Swifts were a different team anyway, literally, as many of the girls I was playing with had moved to play for the Greater Western Sydney (GWS) Giants, another new team in the Suncorp Super Netball.

I had started seeing a guy soon after arriving back in Melbourne, but it was a pretty unsatisfying relationship and I knew he didn't really care about me. However, by that point I didn't care about myself too much either, so why give a shit? It was beginning to feel like I was paying for the multitude of bad decisions I'd made and was continuing to make, from the team I was playing in to the guy I was dating. I suddenly found myself crying every day, and I stopped eating.

The angry outbursts and meltdowns I'd had as a kid started happening on a regular basis when I was alone. Sometimes I'd have to pull the car over when I was driving because I'd start screaming or crying and couldn't stop. I had been mentally strong for so long and had trained my mind to push through, which is why I then struggled in real life. Instead of a sports psychologist, I wondered if I needed a life psychologist to help me learn to be human again. It felt like I was starting to lose control, but I tried to fight it because I knew I had to keep it together. *Just get through the season and then you can crawl into bed and finally let it all go,* I'd tell myself.

Collingwood made the Finals, and in the Semi-Final we came up against the Greater Western Sydney Giants, in front of the huge New South Wales crowd who had once cheered for me when I'd played with the Swifts. After a hard game, we ended up losing by one goal. It was devastating. We had tried so hard, and wanted so badly to win, but just couldn't get it together on the court. We were playing as individuals, not as a team. We were six goals up with five minutes to go and there was no way we should have lost, but we did. We didn't have the key ingredients to success, which are belief and trust – in each other, ourselves and the game plan.

We were dragged back to the change rooms after the game to debrief and the coach made us go over all the reasons why we'd lost. (Sidenote: I think debriefs are always better the following day, once emotions have settled, so you can review the game properly. After a devastating loss in an elimination final, it definitely should not be done straight after the game.) The situation was made even worse when the coach wouldn't let us see our families who had flown up to Sydney for the game, and we were taken straight to the team vans without seeing them or even being able to say goodbye. After a huge loss all you want and need is family and friends to hug you and tell you everything is going to be okay. It felt like the coach wanted to punish us by not letting us see them, and I was beyond furious at the way the whole post-game situation had been handled and made my feelings known. We were adults, yet once again I felt I was being controlled and treated like a child. It reminded me of those final months with the Adelaide Thunderbirds.

All my nerves were on edge and it felt like I was about to snap. Because we didn't make the last two weeks of finals, I had some time before my Aussie team commitments began again, and decided to go to Bali for two weeks by myself as a way to refuel. When I got to Bali, I knew straight away that something wasn't right with me. This was a holiday to escape and be myself, like that time in Byron. But this was different. I got to one of my favourite places in the world and still felt nothing. Then I started behaving more recklessly than I usually would when I knew I had sporting commitments waiting for me back home. I rode a scooter at high speeds through the busy Bali streets and jumped off cliffs when I was terrified of heights. And I was loving the feeling of doing the kind of stuff I would once have been scared to do. I almost hoped something bad would happen when I was doing these high-risk activities, and it nearly did one day when I rode my scooter straight off a bridge. I managed to grab onto the side of the bridge as my scooter plummeted 5 metres onto the concrete below, but instead of shaking me up it just made me feel like James Bond. Completely unfazed, I walked down the ramp, picked up the mangled scooter and kept riding. I had a scuba-diving date with some manta rays!

People who had seen the accident tried to stop me getting back on the scooter, but I wouldn't listen. They must have thought I was a headcase and I wouldn't blame them. At the end of my holiday I took the scooter back to the hire place and the lady took one look at the banged-up scooter and cried, 'YOU THE GIRL THAT DROVE OFF THE BRIDGE!'

Oops. Luckily, I was in Bali, so it only cost me fifty bucks.

I then spent five days in Ubud trying to get back in touch with my spiritual side. I went to yoga classes and sound healing temples. I even went to a spiritual healer. Nothing helped. I cried and cried just like I did when I was at home. I rode the scooter and read some books and continued to journal but I knew something was up; I couldn't get my usual writing flow. I was lonely, I was sad and I just didn't want to be on this planet.

I didn't want to return home after my holiday, but I knew I had no choice. I thought this escape was going to fix me, but it didn't and now I had to face netball and real life again.

When I got back, I went straight to the Australian Team Camp and had to do a wellbeing test, which they call a LEAF-Q. This was something we'd never had to do before. The timing was spooky considering my mental state at the time. We had our bloods taken and did many more wellbeing quizzes, and all of my results came back with alarm bells. I'd lost 8 kilograms since the start of the year and was skin and bone, so plans were immediately put in place to help me put the weight back on, including a food plan that had me eating six times a day. They wanted to help get me better for the tour in a month's time.

My old coach and friend, Lisa Alexander, sat me down and said I needed to learn how to love myself. The whole time she was talking I had an overwhelming urge to tell her where to go. Lisa was only trying to help me, but I didn't care. It was as if I couldn't feel anything anymore and had no idea what love felt like. Angie Bain, the wellbeing coordinator, supported me, too, but I couldn't explain to her what was going on in my head. I didn't understand it myself. All I knew was that I truly believed I'd be an empty and hopeless human being for the rest of my life. However long that was going to be.

Lisa, Angie and our nutritionist Kerry made me a solid step-by-step plan to get me better and put on some weight. When I got back to Melbourne the first thing I did was call my boyfriend to let him know I was unwell and needed to start taking care of myself.

'Well, I'm going out for dinner,' he said. 'You coming or not?'

The penny dropped and I immediately broke it off with him, which was a hard thing to do when I was already feeling shit about myself and alone in the world. I'd only stayed in the relationship because it was a distraction when I wasn't training or playing. It meant that I didn't have to look myself in the face and sit with the broken mess I'd become.

I cried a lot that night and didn't sleep, stressing because I had training with the Diamonds the next day. I knew I wasn't feeling mentally strong enough to train, but I didn't feel comfortable calling the coach either. Our relationship was still rocky and although she knew things weren't right with me, she didn't know how to help, nor should she have.

I called our physio and asked if she could reach out to the coach and ask about me having the day off training. When the physio called back, she said it was a no. The coach expected me to show up. I couldn't understand. I had just gone through a break-up and asked to have a day off from training, something I hadn't done since my first season with the team in 2011, and she'd said no. Maybe it was because I hadn't called her myself? Obviously, I wasn't in the right headspace and hadn't followed the proper process in asking for the day off, but was that really why? I don't know because I didn't ask and never have. I don't need to know.

The fact is that no-one, including myself, knew how bad things were for me at that point and that I was suffering from severe depression. I don't blame anyone, including the coach, for what happened next. There was a long line of triggers leading up to that point, but this was just the one that finally pushed me over the edge. I was full of hatred and resentment at having given up so much but receiving no emotional support.

I sucked it up and went to training that day. I walked out angry and resentful without saying goodbye to anyone. Little did I know that would be my last session as an Australian Diamond.

When I got home afterwards, I lost the plot. I crawled into bed and sobbed for hours. The Sharni who had once been so mentally strong, like a machine, felt a million miles away from the person

I was now. I couldn't accept how weak I had become, and I was ashamed.

My phone rang beside me but the thought of talking to anyone at all gave me so much anxiety that I picked up my phone, threw it against the wall and screamed. I was in so much pain. My heart and head hurt, and the empty feeling in my gut was unbearable. I wanted to tear my hair out and punch myself in the face to take away the emotional pain I was feeling inside, just like when I was a kid and would punch the ground to let go of the frustration inside me.

Physical pain would have been a relief at that point. Hurting myself seemed like a better option than sitting with the emotional turmoil I was in.

CHAPTER TWENTY-FOUR

THE ROAD BACK

It was July 2017 and I had reached the peak of my depression. I was completely numb. I hated not feeling anything, having no emotion. But I didn't feel like I had a choice. This was the person I had become.

The only thing keeping me around was knowing how much suffering I would cause my family if I wasn't around anymore. I remained curled up in bed.

I don't want to do this anymore, I can't do this anymore, I can't be in this world anymore.

The words played on a loop inside my head, but out of nowhere a new voice, one I hadn't heard before, spoke up. *Get your phone. You need help. You can't do this on your own anymore.*

I got out of bed, picked up my smashed phone and dialled Angie's number. In between sobs, I confessed that I wasn't okay. She said she knew and had been waiting for the call. Her words immediately calmed me. Within ten minutes of getting off the phone to me, she called me back to tell me she'd arranged for me to see a psychiatrist the next day.

I didn't know what to expect going to a psychiatrist. I had once refused to see one when I knew I wasn't depressed, but this time was different; this time I knew I needed help. I felt relieved that I had conceded defeat to my demons; I didn't have to pretend I was okay anymore, I could fall. But still, I didn't know what I was in for and I was nervous as I walked into the psychiatry clinic. It wasn't as scary as I thought, not dissimilar to any other doctor's surgery or even a physio, with friendly women at the front desk. I waited for my psychiatrist to come out and he called me into the room. Ranjit was calm, had a sense of reassurance about him and I felt safe in his presence. He introduced himself and asked a few questions, but it didn't take him long to understand me or my personality. I was understood, which is something that was a rarity in my life up until that point. Before long, Ranjit started describing the symptoms of depression to me.

'You're unmotivated, lack energy and don't feel like doing anything.'

'Yep.'

'You feel low all the time, you're numb and don't experience emotions.'

'Yep.'

'You feel socially awkward because you struggle to have conversations.'

'Yep.'

'Your brain isn't firing properly, so you're extremely forgetful or your memory may not be working well at all.'

'Yep.' The realisation of how sick I was kicked in for the first time. 'Fuck. I'm really bad.'

Don't get me wrong, I knew I was sick, but I didn't know how severe it was, and there was still a long way to go to before I found this out, too. I'd known something wasn't right for a while, but I had no idea how bad things were because I'd kept myself busy for so long. Pushing through, getting through. *We just need to get through.* But when does it end if we don't address it ourselves?

'There are different levels of depression,' he said, 'but you tick all the boxes and it's quite severe. But it's okay now because I'm here for you and we'll get through this.'

Ranjit went on to explain the science of the brain. He unpacked my personality and the problems I'd been facing, which had a lot to do with me putting a mask on whenever I was in the netball environment. I wasn't being my authentic self when I was there, and constantly feared judgement. I was an introverted extrovert. No-one could have guessed that part of me was an introvert because of my ability to be loud and put on a show. But this kind of behaviour didn't recharge my batteries as a human. Just because I was good at being extroverted, didn't mean it was good for me. It was actually extremely detrimental as I wasn't serving the part of me that needed 'me time', the introverted Sharni. Being 'on' all the time had worn me down as I was always the one who was expected to be upbeat and turn the mood in a game. My mind was telling me it had had enough of that and wanted a quiet day with no judgement. Usually when I was quiet, I'd hear, *'Gee, Sharni's quiet today. Must be something wrong with her.'* There was nothing wrong with this expectation, except that as someone who felt like I was constantly being judged, it just created more judgement on myself.

But there wasn't actually anything wrong with me when I was quiet, I was just having a quiet day and this extra judgement on top of all the other expectations had taken its toll. It's important to be aware of the expectations we put on ourselves. Are they realistic? Sometimes, but often not, and this was definitely the case for me.

It was an immense relief to finally sit with someone and unpack and verbalise what was going on in my mind and have them lead the way. The best part of all was that my psychiatrist and my new psychologist that I had started seeing didn't seem to care if I played netball again or not. They just wanted me to be a healthy, happy human. I could have honest conversations with them without being judged for having certain thoughts and feelings.

Prior to these sessions, I was starting to think I'd turned into a mega-bitch who was socially awkward and had lost all motivation for life. I assumed this was just part of being an adult and that I wouldn't find an environment I felt I belonged in ever again. But the more I uncovered, the more I knew what I needed to work on to start to try and heal myself. There was a lot of leftover stuff from Melbourne, Adelaide, and the Diamonds. A backlog of netball shit in general. The psychiatrist taught me that there will always be stuff that will come up, but the best path to healing is to let go – not to try to figure out why you are triggered, but to accept it and move on. I could then make informed choices based on what I have learned serves me as a human and stay true to my values. This is what *truly* makes us happy.

A good friend and amazing coach Joe Pane has an excellent quote: 'We don't need motivation to live our values more than we need motivation to breathe.' I love this because it's true. You can't make someone love something or enjoy something; they do or they don't. By knowing what you love, you can make informed choices, rather than making a decision based on what you *think* you should do. Doing the latter can be a slippery slope to unhappiness.

Once I learned this, I understood it. However, I found it hard to know how I was going to learn to feel again. Being with myself and by myself, I was forced to stare into the face of the loneliness, something I'd avoided doing for years. Over those sessions I spent a lot of time crying as I attempted to get to the bottom of the hopeless pit I'd found myself in. I felt as if I could only start to bounce back once I hit rock bottom, but I had no idea how far I would have to fall.

My family and friends checked in on me a lot. I was still living with Mel and another friend, Sarah, and they all did their best to care for me. I was so grateful to them for loving and supporting me for who I was. Angie, my psychiatrist Ranjit and my psychologist Kate were my rocks, too. They all saved me, but more importantly, empowered me to take action.

Once I decided to take a break, I still had it in my mind that I was taking the break to get better – not to be a healthier human, but so I could play in the Commonwealth Games. Once again, my goal was netball, not life. Of course, I had a plan. There was *always* a plan … and that was the problem.

I'll take three months off and then come back, I thought. *That will give me enough time to get ready for the Commonwealth Games in April 2018.*

After eight weeks of therapy, I was facing my demons and had finally hit rock bottom, and there I was thinking I could take three months off and be back playing netball. However, when the three months were up, I was still at the bottom of that pit and hadn't yet started climbing out. I just couldn't see a light at the end of the tunnel. I have no idea how other people work and live with depression. I do understand how a lot of people don't survive depression and that makes me so sad. The tunnel of loneliness and emptiness isn't somewhere anyone wants to spend too much time in, and most of those who haven't been there at all just don't understand what it's like.

Even today, I don't take one second of my Netball Australia sick leave for granted. It meant that I could afford to take that time off to get better, and it saved my life. If I hadn't had the company's financial help and support, I don't know where I would have ended up. It was a horrible time and I'm so grateful I had help to get me through to the other side. I was in no state to do any work of any kind and I don't know what would have happened if I had to push through that and keep dealing with life.

It felt like it took such a long time to get there. When I say 'there', I mean a place where I could cope with living day-to-day life and be okay with the way my mind ticks.

By November, after four months of respite, I was starting to see some improvement in my moods and all through November and December I got back to doing things I remembered loving. I rode my horse, I hung out with my gorgeous little nieces and my family, I went for nature walks, I got my scuba licence and started hitting up live music gigs again. All these activities started to bring joy and happiness back into my life again. I drank here and there, but mostly avoided alcohol because, well, it's a depressant.

I started having moments where I'd feel things, which was progress, but I knew I'd be in trouble if I tried to make my way back to netball. This wasn't just because I wasn't in the right headspace to play, but also because I'd decided I'd had enough. For real this time. I didn't want to play anymore. I had no motivation to go back. Despite taking time off to get better for the Commonwealth Games, after five months of weekly therapy with Ranjit and Kate, they had helped me start setting goals to be happy and healthy in life, and with this, any drive to achieve anything else in netball melted away.

During my time off I'd had time to reflect on what I'd achieved in netball for the first time in my life. *For God's sake, Layton*, I thought. *You've done so much. Can't you see that?*

Slowly I came to realise that I was proud of myself and that there was nothing left for me to achieve. I had no drive or desire to train anymore. There was only one goal left dangling in front of me. Because of my mental conditioning, there was still a pull to try and get back for the Commonwealth Games. I didn't want to leave any stone unturned, which meant playing for one last year to make sure I didn't regret leaving.

I went back to training in January, and in my first week back I had trials for the Commonwealth Games. Selection processes have changed over the years and instead of reading the team out in front of everyone, you now get a phone call after you leave Camp. My phone rang and Lisa advised me that I wouldn't be selected in the team or as a training partner for the Commonwealth Games. I was shattered. I knew I hadn't trained much, but figured I'd have four months to get back to the fitness required. I'd needed the Australian team as a driver for me to keep playing netball because after the previous season I was extremely hesitant to get back to playing in club land again. Once I missed out on the Games team, all my motivation was gone.

I decided to have a night out with my housemate to let off some steam before knuckling down to 'netball time' again. Sarah and I headed to the St Kilda Festival and soon ended up at a crowded bar. It was my first time drinking in a while, and I was having a great time when I spotted a group of guys and girls who seemed to be having the night of their lives. Their loud, fun vibes caught my attention and I started chatting with a couple of them. Sarah was ready to go home by then, so I sent her on her way and stayed to hang with my new group of mates.

One of the guys in the group caught my eye. He was six-foot-six, gorgeous, covered in tatts from head to toe and seemed like a bit of a loose cannon.

Sharni, I told myself sternly. *This bloke is not for you.*

But when we started chatting, I found out that he was raising money for three charities – Peter Mac, Beyond Blue and MS. Once he'd raised $70,000, he and his mates planned to hike up Mount Everest. Although he knew it was a very different experience, he wanted to put himself through something tough and challenging, like so many people facing illnesses did every day. I was stunned listening to this intelligent, thoughtful and caring tattooed bikie dude. His name was Luke and we soon opened up to each other about our respective mental demons. We were connecting on more levels than just the physical (or maybe that was just me) and I loved talking with him. The night wore on and at one point he whipped off his top, swung it around like a lasso and was promptly kicked out of the pub. As I watched him leaving, I thought, *That's my future husband right there.*

Outside, I asked for his number so I could transfer money to his charity … and maybe even call him sometime for another catch-up (*smooth, I know*). Later that week I scored free tickets to Pink Floyd and invited Luke along.

'Meet me at eight, this isn't a date,' I'd said.

I liked the guy but was wary of getting myself in trouble with the wrong guy again. After the last relationship I'd made a list of my values and I wanted to be sure Luke checked all the boxes before he got the tick of approval.

This all went out the window the moment I saw him. He was even more gorgeous sober, and I fell. Hard.

We chatted all through the concert, and at the end of the night he walked me past his Harley Davidson (hot) and back to my car for a goodnight kiss. The following night we had another date and I sent my sister a message after it that read, *'I've found my soulmate.'*

From that day on, Luke and I were inseparable. My family met him and instantly loved him. They could see that he was my best mate and the love of my life. Luke had been scuba diving his whole life and once I got my diving licence, I found time underwater to be therapeutic and calm. He promised to teach me a thing or two, and even took me to his childhood holiday spot, Wilsons Promontory. I'd never met anyone like him. He was beautiful, thoughtful, caring and strong, not only in his body, but also in his mind. Our relationship just grew stronger and stronger, and for the first time in my life I realised I was truly happy and fulfilled in a personal relationship. I could finally see that my previous relationships had all failed because they were relationships of convenience, not of love. Once I learned to love myself, and be happy with who I was, I could finally be part of a successful and functioning relationship.

I was so proud of myself for getting back to netball training and continuing my journey back from depression and having Luke's support and love helped so much. He didn't know I played netball when we first met, and he didn't care either. He just loved me for me. This alone helped keep me stable when I felt I wasn't being supported at the club after my return. Don't get me wrong, they absolutely tried to help and gave me training sessions off when I was struggling. But it wasn't the time off I needed, it was emotional and moral support, and that's what I didn't receive, as I don't think they knew how to provide it.

On my first training session back with Collingwood, I stepped onto the baseline of the court for warm-up for what felt like the millionth time in my life, and immediately thought, *If I have to do one more warm-up, I'm going to punch myself in the face.* In that moment, I knew I was done. I had no passion left, I didn't want to be there and I knew this was going to be the hardest season of my life to get through. I felt that my coach and I still didn't respect each other, and things soon went from bad to worse. We clashed more than ever, because I now knew who I was again, and I started sticking up for myself and questioning why things were how they were rather than just going with it. I had done so much work on myself; I wasn't going to let my last season of netball take me back to square one. I never wanted to go through six months of hell like I had *ever* again.

My teammates were pressuring me to live and act by the team rules, which meant staying quiet and doing what I was told even when I knew it was wrong. These 'rules' didn't allow me to be myself and conflicted with the work I was doing to get my mental health back. Elite sport isn't the best place for someone who is struggling with their mental health, and the right processes just weren't in place to give me the support I needed. If a player took six months off to recover from a knee injury, they would be introduced back into playing slowly so as not to make it worse. I don't see any difference with depression. Your mind also needs time to heal and learn how to take information in again. But no-one seemed to understand this, and it was hard to explain, so I was thrown straight back in the deep end. I broke down crying many times in front of my teammates in those first few weeks back, and soon it just became the norm again.

It was still preseason when the 2018 Gold Coast Commonwealth Games rolled around. My parents had expected me to make it so had already booked accommodation and had decided to go up during the games even though I wasn't playing. I was torn about whether to go or not. I wanted to support the team, but at the same time I was so heartbroken that I wasn't in it that I just didn't know if I could cope being there when I was still so fragile. First World problem, but it was the first Australian team since 2012 that I hadn't been picked for.

I finally decided that I would go, but once I arrived in Queensland, I couldn't bring myself to go to a game. I knew people would be lovely and want to come over and say hello to me, but I wanted to stay under the radar. Truthfully I didn't know how I would react being in the crowd, either; no-one wants a public breakdown!

When the Final between England and Australia came, instead of going to the game, my friends Jodie and Bec and I went to the casino to watch it in the beer garden on the big screen. What I didn't know was that Netball Australia had hired the casino's outdoor area for netball fans, so coincidentally the netball family surrounded me anyway, which turned out to be a beautiful way to spend the day. It's fair to say the netball fans were pretty stoked that I was watching the game with them and I was grateful for their love and support. We cheered and egged on the girls during the game, but were getting nervous as England started coming back at Australia. When we lost by a goal, silence fell upon us all. I was devastated and cried into my hands; everyone was respectful and gave me space. I felt so bad for the team and just so helpless because I hadn't been able to go out on that court with them and contribute to the game. To say it broke my heart would be an understatement and made me want to make a comeback – almost.

The best part of the Commonwealth Games was that I could interact with the fans in a way that wouldn't distract the team, because I was no longer in the team. So, the night before the Final I'd announced on Instagram that I'd wear the England dress if they won. But Australia had lost and I knew I'd have to keep my promise, especially when I was inundated with messages from UK fans holding me to it. I was mortified, not just because I have major issues about wearing England's colours, but because I knew my Aussie teammates would be furious with me.

The following week I appeared on the Fox Footy show *Bounce* and the boys on the show asked me to wear the England dress. I decided it would be a good opportunity to get it over and done with, especially in a humorous environment like a footy show. Unfortunately, my club teammates got wind of it and told me it would be completely inappropriate to wear the dress, saying they were so disappointed in me for saying it in the first place.

I tried to explain that I worked in the entertainment industry, and that this was just a media stunt to draw in attention around the game and they shouldn't take it personally, but they didn't understand. I was just a shit person; how dare I do such a thing? I also knew that bringing up netball on a footy show with an audience of two hundred thousand could potentially bring more people over to our sport, but no-one saw it that way. I had Australian and English players all messaging to say how disappointed they were in me, so I told the *Bounce* guys that I wouldn't be able to wear the dress.

Jason Dunstall was gobsmacked. 'Are you kidding? It's a joke!' he said. 'Don't worry, Sharns, even if they don't have your back, I do. You're a part of our team and I'll wear the dress for you.'

He wasn't lying, either. Jason went on air on Sunday night wearing an England netball dress that the show had made for him and I was so touched. My own sport didn't have my back, but this legitimate AFL legend did. He was my new hero. It was the first time I wondered if it might be possible to get into a different sporting environment, one that accepted my personality the way it was.

The girls were already mad at me for the whole saga. Then, we were told by the leadership group that we were doing too much media and we needed to back off. But I was the only one working in the media, so it was clearly directed at me. I didn't understand, but I'd been in this situation enough times before that it stopped being a fight worth having. I just had to get through the rest of the year until I could be me, and do me, with freedom.

The season finally kicked off where it finished after losing the Semi-Final: negatively. And that was the theme for the rest of the year.

The players couldn't seem to shake their fears, as we were dragged during training sessions and games if we threw a bad pass or didn't catch the ball, which, in turn, meant we missed a lot of passes and dropped a lot of balls. No-one felt safe in their position and that was reflected in the way we were playing. The defence end was trying to stay positive, especially April, Braz and I.

We would pretend to make pizzas with Italian accents when we were doing the long court drills to keep each other sane and have a bit of fun with it. I would yell to Braz, 'Brazzy, I'm sending you the base!' and throw the ball. Then she would go, 'April, there's a tomato paste coming your way!' and April would then pass it on to whoever was next with her favourite pizza topping. Then if the shooters threw it out of court, we would say 'Oh, bit too much chilli on that one, shooters!' I don't think they found it as funny as we did, but we did what we had to do to get through the training sessions.

By the time we were halfway through the season, I'd had a gutful. I had an altercation with the coach right before a game and after that, she didn't play me. I was continually benched for the remainder of the year. As far as I was concerned, the year couldn't be over fast enough. I was done with being micromanaged and told how I should act and be. I wanted to be free of all that. I know I'd made life harder for myself by talking back, but I was thirty years old and refused to be treated like a child any longer.

'Stop trying to explain to the team what you're going through, Sharni,' my psychologist said. 'It's like a shark tank. You're in the tank with them and you do something that annoys them, which you didn't mean, and they bite off your arm. You get out of the tank, but when you jump back in to tell them it wasn't what you meant, they bite off your other arm. These people don't understand you, and they don't need to, so stop trying to make them.'

This analogy was great, and finally opened my eyes to what was happening. She was right. I had kept trying to explain myself over and over to these people, to tell them what I was going through and why I was like I was, but they kept misinterpreting what I was saying. Trying to make them understand was pointless, and the only one it was hurting was me. Through the final weeks of the season I continued working with my psychiatrist and psychologist and we all agreed that netball was no longer a healthy place for me to be. I had always loved the joy that playing sport brought me, but it had all got too serious and there was no fun in it anymore for me.

Although I had some support in the team, it wasn't enough to keep me in the game.

There were only a few games left in the season when I met with the CEO of the club.

'Mark, I want to retire,' I said, 'and I know the playing group hates it when the attention is on me, so I don't want to make a fuss about it. I just want to play the last game and walk away. I'm telling you so you don't get a shock when I don't re-sign with the club next year.'

Mark was surprised, to say the least, but he understood.

'I respect your decision,' he said, 'but please have a think about letting us celebrate your career at our last home game. We'd like to say goodbye to you, and I know many of your fans would, too.'

In the end I decided he was right. I'd had an amazing career, one I was proud of, and I'd always cared about my fans. In fact, that year I'd gotten in trouble a lot for seeming to care more about the fans than I did my team, which may have been true. Throughout my whole career my fans had always supported and loved me. They never judged me for being who I was, and this was why I loved them.

And so, the Sharni show began. I tapped back into my bubbly self and made an effort to enjoy the last two weeks of the season. The club wanted to film the moment I announced my retirement to the team. I knew that the footage would be hilarious, since the girls hated the media, and the fact that I was making it all about me would have just peeved them off even more. But I didn't care by that stage, so I did it anyway.

Coming up to the last game of the season, the club announced they weren't renewing the coach's contract, but it felt to me that she had already given up. As a departure gift, the last two training sessions were by far the worst. We did shuttles and got absolutely physically smashed, so by the time we had to play we were mentally and physically cooked. Because of this, we lost by thirty-two goals. To add insult to injury, myself and two other retiring players found ourselves on the bench in our last game. Ever.

We just looked at each other and said, 'Thank fuck we're retiring,' and burst out laughing. It had been a long, hard year for all of us, but it was probably the first time we'd all been on the same page. In a way I guess it was fitting that I finished my career the way it started, doing time on the pine.

It was 4 August 2018 when I played my last game of netball and emotionally farewelled my amazing supporters. After that last game, the relief of it all being over was next level. Finally, I felt free and happy. Not a single part of me was sad about retiring. Luke had moved in with me, and I was spending more time with my family and doing things I loved. Things were finally going my way and I felt hopeful and excited about the future.

Plus, it turned out that I wasn't done with elite women's sport. Not just yet.

Times you should apologise #86

When you break your teammate's foot
because you're so unco.
(SORRY, BRITT)

CHAPTER TWENTY-FIVE

FREEDOM

Luke works interstate as an electrician and instrument technician, doing two weeks on and one week off, so it was easier for him to move in with me early on in our relationship. We'd only been going out for three months but I knew in my heart and soul that it was the right decision, and it meant we could spend the whole week together when he was home. I knew pretty soon after we got together that I was going to marry him, but I definitely wasn't expecting his proposal when it came on New Year's Day 2019, eleven months after we started going out.

Luke told me he wanted to ride his Harley Davidson down to meet me on our family holiday to Phillip Island because he wanted to have the bike for rides once we were there. In truth, he wanted to ride past Mum and Dad's house in Bonbeach and ask for Dad's permission to marry me. Mum, Kara, the kids and I were already down there waiting for the boys to join us. Luke told me later that he was nervous as hell, and was suddenly regretting his decision to ride the Harley as he rocked up to my parents' house. Who knew if this man would agree to his daughter marrying a biker boy?

As if Luke wasn't nervous enough, it took twenty minutes before Dad finally answered the door as he'd been out the back mowing the lawn and hadn't heard Luke knocking. Thankfully, Dad told Luke he'd be very happy about him marrying his daughter, and a relieved Luke set off to Phillip Island to pop the big question.

When Luke arrived he told me he wanted to spend the day with me, so we jumped on the Harley, went out for breakfast and had a kick of the footy. Then we headed for Inverloch to catch up with Luke's mates, but on the way Luke pulled the bike into Oaks Beach for an adventure. Like anything with Luke, there was no set path, so we bush-bashed our way through the scrub and found ourselves at the edge of the cliff. Once out there, Luke put on some music, which happened to be Pink Floyd (from our first date) and as I went to grab his jumper to sit on, he lunged at me. I didn't know what was going on until he was on one knee and I had nearly knocked the ring over the cliff. Half-shocked at what had just unfolded in front of me, I couldn't get the words out to say, 'Yes!' so I just cried until Luke said 'So, is that a yes?' I just nodded my head and hugged and kissed him.

I felt like the happiest girl in the world; I was engaged to the man of my dreams. I later found out that Luke had had every black diamond he could find flown in from around Australia before choosing the best one for the ring, which he designed himself. It's an absolute boss ring and I love it. More importantly, the day Luke proposed was the tenth anniversary of his best mate and cousin Carl's death. Luke and Carl had been so close and when Carl committed suicide it left a giant hole in Luke's life. He'd been carrying the pain and heartache of Carl's death for so long, and decided that he wanted to use the anniversary as a turning point in his life and make it a positive. He could now incorporate memories of Carl into this new chapter of his life, and I knew how much it meant to him, and therefore, to me. It was such a special day, and Kilcunda and Oaks Beach are now two of our favourite spots together. It was also the perfect start to the year, and the post-netball chapter of my life.

After my final netball season had wrapped up in 2018, a member of the netball team's leadership group apologised to me for the way I'd been treated. It would have been good to hear that and have their support while I was still playing, but it was nice to have someone acknowledge what I'd been through. I appreciated it, but I wasn't ready for it to be water under the bridge quite yet, and had no intention of ever putting myself back in an environment like that again.

All the time I'd been struggling to connect with my teammates during that final season of netball, there was another bunch of players who were keeping me sane: the footballers. We all trained in the same vicinity and I thought they were the funniest group of chicks I'd ever met. Every time I rocked up for netball training, I'd sit and talk to them until I had to go start my warm-up on the netball court.

I'd walk past the AFLW Collingwood coach's office and jokingly call out, 'G'day, Wayne! Remember to keep a spot open for me next year!'

Now, with netball over, I started to think, *Why not give it a crack?* My netball teammate, Ash Brazill, also played AFLW, proving that it was possible to play a different sport outside of netball. A few weeks after retiring, I gave Wayne a call to see if he might be willing to take my joke seriously.

'How about we go have a kick and then I can assess taking you on or not?'

So, we met up for a kick and I was okay, but not great. However, I could mark the ball, thanks to my netball hands, and between this skill and my elite sport experience that I would be able to share with the team, it was enough for Wayne to take me on.

At the age of thirty I was a rookie again, and I was pumped!

Before starting football, I played netball in one last retirement tour to the United Kingdom for their Fast5 tournament. More than anything, I wanted to say goodbye to the 'Sharni Army' support base I had there after playing for Australia over the past three years.

I played for Surrey Storm and had a brilliant time. For me, that experience was what netball is all about – pure enjoyment, love of the game and supporting one another. Afterwards, I was so glad that I'd done it and could walk away from the game remembering how much fun netball could be and what a great sport it is.

Harking back to my Commonwealth Games promise of donning the red England dress, I told my English fans that I'd wear it on the last day of the tournament. And I did. Some people found it funny, others were pissed off, but 'those that mind don't matter, and those that matter don't mind.'

I continued my retirement tour to Scotland and Dubai where I ran clinics for fans who had supported me throughout my whole career. I felt lucky and grateful to be able to do this and was so glad I'd decided to come.

I returned to Melbourne for my first training session with the Collingwood Football Club, feeling free and happy. My teammates were awesome, and I loved training with them. There was no judgement or jealousy, and no-one cared if I worked in the media. Feeling accepted for who I was a refreshing change and, in return, I wanted to give this team my all.

But it was a tough transition, and a month into training I was sure I'd never get a game. I was hopeless. I could mark when I wasn't tired, but after running 6–8 kilometres on the training track, I wasn't marking shit. Also, I was worried about my awkward running style. I'd been able to get away with it on the netball court's 150 square metres, but it would be pretty obvious when I had to run back and forth across a huge footy oval. I had an awkward run, an awkward kick and … well, an awkward everything!

I was at the club one day when Tarkyn Lockyer, Collingwood legend and an AFL men's coach who'd been helping out with our training, pulled me aside.

'Sharni, how do you think you're going?'

'Pretty shit, Tarks.'

'Yeah, I think so, too.'

Wowza, I thought. *Harsh much?*

'What's the go?' he said. 'You're the hardest-working athlete I know, but you haven't put in any extra effort. Meet me here tomorrow at lunchtime and we'll start doing some extra work to make you better.'

'Okay, Tarks, thank you … I think.'

Tarks is a demanding human being and would have made a great army sergeant. He's truthful because he wants the best for you, and I was touched and felt honoured that he'd cared enough about me to have that (very honest) conversation and offer to help me in his free time.

Tarks taught me how to kick, do bodywork to free me up for the mark, pick up ground balls, lead differently and compete with players in the air. Basically, he taught me everything I now know skills-wise. He pushed me to my limits, and I loved every second. I knew I was still an average player, but at least I managed to get a gig for Round One.

My first game of football was a roller-coaster. I was so excited to play, but also incredibly nervous. My mate, Ash Braz, presented me with my jumper before the game and I started to bawl my eyes out. To have the people in the football world embrace me and my personality, after years of feeling like a misfit, was overwhelming but felt so good.

The good feelings quickly disappeared as soon as I got out on the field because I felt like I was terrible and looked out of place. It was SO hard, and I had no idea what I was doing. I was knackered from running so much, I gave away a fifty and knocked out a teammate who was our only goal scorer. I played so badly, and when we lost by three points, I was devastated at having let the team down. I knew I had done the best I could, but it was still embarrassing.

I was also copping criticism from the public about how hopeless I was. But I knew from the work I'd been doing with my psychs that outside opinions don't mean anything. I knew where I was at, and as long as my coach and team were happy with me, nothing else mattered. I think the reason I was okay with being so bad at footy was because of what I'd been through in the past couple of years. Before my breakdown, I couldn't deal with the idea of being anything but great at whatever I did. Whether it was playing netball or appearing on a TV show, I had to be 'great'. I was a perfectionist, so being average just wasn't good enough. But going through depression and working with my psychs, I learned that I didn't need to be great at everything anymore. So, football was a new challenge for me. Most importantly, I did it because it was fun and I enjoyed it, and I was finally able to challenge my perfectionistic traits by being the worst at something on the public stage. I was playing purely for the love of a sport and not because there were any expectations on me to be 'great'.

Luke had once been a bit of a hero at the Morwell Footy Club and never tires of reminding me that he appeared in the *La Trobe Valley Express* numerous times. Clearly, I had a lot to live up to having such a talented future husband! But in all seriousness, Luke helped me heaps with my ruck work, and I also stayed focused on improving one skill at a time with Tarks.

My first AFLW season was from January through to April in 2019, and from April to September that year I played VFLW, which was great for further improving my skills after a year of training and applying myself to this new sport. I used the application skills I'd learned through netball, doing the hours of work and watching people who played the same position as me, always learning and adapting. I soon realised that it was possible to work and train hard at a sport AND have fun. In fact, it was making me play even better.

When we won the Premiership for VFLW, I was so stoked and thought, *Holy shit, I've won a Premiership in footy in my first year! Maybe I'll just retire!* Eddie Maguire promised us he'd put a painting of the first Premiership-winning women's team in the boardroom. We're still waiting, Ed!

By the start of 2020, I'd transformed into a stronger and better player than I was a year earlier. I was a dominant ruck and had reduced my two-kilometre time trial from eight minutes and forty seconds to eight minutes and ten seconds. The extra fitness allowed me to play over the whole ground and made me a force to be reckoned with. When I scored my first goal I was over the moon and did an aeroplane victory run in a spontaneous outbreak of pure joy. I literally could not believe that I had kicked a goal. After my first year of hopelessness I really never thought it would happen, so when I took a netball-style grab in front of the goal that day, I was beside myself! It was an amazing feeling. After being a defender my whole sporting career, I was finally kicking goals!

A year of solid improvement from the whole team, which resulted in the club making Finals for the first time, had many contributing factors. With new coaches, an improved training ethos and game strategy, along with the personal development I continued to do outside of training with Brodie Grundy (who is an absolute gun), I earned myself the title of All-Australian Ruck two years into playing this new sport.

It's funny how it works out. Previously I had put so much time and effort into achieving things, and that had made me miserable. Now I was the happiest I had ever been, playing the sport to help lift those around me and pass on the elite performance behaviours I had learned in netball to football. It was amazing to see that focusing on what made me happy could still bring me success in my career.

I had worked my arse off to improve so much, but I couldn't have gotten there without my teammates. They encouraged and pushed me all season, nicknaming me Bambi because of how uncoordinated I was, and I understood that this was a term of endearment, not sledging. My footy teammates understood my personality, and there was a lot of piss-taking among us all. It was all in good fun and, as I'm a shit-stirrer from way back, I loved the fact that they felt comfortable enough to do the same with me.

I was constantly inspired by my teammates and how hard they worked, especially Jaimee Lambert. She always pulls me into line during a game, and on the training track, and I never want to let her down. Brianna Davey is a gun who I work hard to get the ball to, because I know she'll do something better with it than I could. Britt Bonnici is a next-level demon who puts her head over every ball. I've never seen anyone want the ball more, in any sport. Stacey Livingstone is the best defender I've ever seen. No-one is getting the ball if they're near her, and she makes all her opponents look useless. I could say positive comments like this about every single one of my teammates, which is what makes us such a great team. They push and inspire me to be better every day, and I plan to keep playing footy as long as my body lets me.

I also enjoy the fact that AFLW isn't yet a full-time sport because it allows me to have a life and work as well. I don't want to be a full-time athlete anymore and I know I need a balanced lifestyle to be at my best, which the AFLW allows me to do.

That's not to say I wouldn't like a longer season, and to be paid professionally like I was in netball, but with more games and a longer season, I know that will eventually come. The AFL boys don't hit their straps until Round Ten. Remember how crap the quality of the game was at the start of 2020 when the boys were adjusting to sixteen-minute quarters (which is what we play)?

Just imagine how different AFL would be if the season

finished after seven of those games. But after Round Seventeen, the boys are flying. This is why the AFLW needs to build up to more games before they start introducing new teams. We just start building momentum after seven rounds, and then, BOOM, season over. I have faith that we'll get there, but hopefully it won't take as long as it did to get the league started in the first place.

Football and netball are very different games. Netball is highly demanding on your mind, and you need to train and play at 100 per cent intensity all the time because you get more rest during a game. Football is more physically demanding, but you can't push yourself 100 per cent or you'll cook yourself in the first quarter and won't have enough energy for the rest of the game. It's a different challenge in every way and I love it. It's also showed me that you're never too old to start, and never too old to finish. I know now that I will never give up playing sport, no matter what level it's at or what it is. I love sport for the community it brings and for the skills and support it provides when you have nowhere else to turn in life. I love that it is an escape from day-to-day life, whether you feel like you need that escape or not.

At the start of 2020 I was still playing football and doing the Fox Footy show, *Bounce*, and those boys had become like family to me. It's a great environment and the guys all have such a wicked sense of humour and always have my back.

After COVID-19 hit and our season was cut short (and wasn't it just an absolute shitfight for everybody?), I felt so lucky to get my first job outside of being an athlete in many years as the head of netball at a private school in Melbourne. I absolutely love being part of a school community, where I can pay forward what I have learned in my career to the next generation.

Did I find this year hard in Melbourne after not one, but two lockdowns? Abso-fucking-lutely. I had no-one that lived in my 5-kilometre radius and my beautiful fiancé still works away so I was alone 90 per cent of the time. There were days that I absolutely lost my shit. So, what was the difference between now and 'back then'? Because I don't judge my personality traits anymore, I'm okay if I have a bad day or two (or three). I ride it out. I give myself time and space, I do things I love like riding my horse, going for nature walks, doing yoga or doing breathing classes to help get me back in check, then away I go. I found it important to keep myself occupied, so I was lucky to use this time to write you this book, but I also had the time to do something I've wanted to do for years but never had the time; I created the Sharni Layton Sport Academy for Netball and Women's Football. If it wasn't for having the time off, I never would have been able to do the groundwork for a start-up, and I'm so proud of myself for getting this off the ground. These programs are about improving skills, but more importantly they are about creating physical and mental strength that will help adolescent girls and boys in any endeavour they choose, inside or outside of sport. I finally have the time to explore creative projects like this, projects that make me happy. More importantly, I can't wait to marry the man of my dreams.

Luke and I had only been together for eleven months when we got engaged, and our wedding was planned for April 2020 in Hawaii. When COVID-19 hit, we decided to postpone and reschedule the wedding, as did millions of other people around the world. But once again, the silver lining was that we ended up using the money we were refunded to finally become real adults and purchase our first home together. Having all of this great life stuff and work to occupy me during this time didn't make the Melbourne lockdown any easier; however, I knew I would be grateful looking back at the time I had to do what we did, and I am. My support network also helped me tremendously. One of the most helpful things I've learned is to surround myself with people who lift me up, not bring me down. It can be hard to distance yourself from negative nellies, but it's also important. There are also many people I have lost touch with over the years, and it's got nothing to do with them personally. But I have such strong friendships that I didn't put enough time into over the years because I spread myself so thin. Now I minimise the number of people I surround myself with, so I can give those people the time that they deserve. No-one more so than Luke Norder, who is my rock and soulmate. We adventure together, laugh together and sometimes even cry together. Every day we challenge each other to be better humans, and to be better at what we do. We talk through everything and never leave anything unsaid because our love for each other is more important than any stupid issue we might have a spat about. He empowers me and makes me feel like a queen. I am so proud of the man he is, what he has overcome and who he has become.

I love that people influence our lives, as we do theirs. Never forget how far a smile can spread or how kind words can make someone feel. For teaching me this, I'm so grateful to my fans and support networks, and if you are reading this book, then that is you.

You might have been someone who has followed me on some part of my journey, whether it was as a youngster in Melbourne trying to make my way, through my breakout years in Adelaide, during my rise to 'netballer fame' in Sydney, my disappearance for six months, my retirement or my code-hopping to the AFLW. You might be someone I had a conversation with somewhere along the way, maybe on one of the hundred aeroplane flights I've been on. Or you might have come along to a game, or switched on your TV to support women in sport. Whoever you are, I thank you.

Thank you for being a part of my journey, but more broadly, thank you for being a part of the rise of women's sport. We are in a greater position now than we have ever been, but I want you to know the job is not done. I ask you to continue being a part of sell-out crowds, turning your TVs on to watch women play and get our ratings up. We've got some work to do if we want to catch up to the sporting beasts like the AFL, NRL or whatever giant men's league is played where you are.

You guys are my community, and community and connection are what life is all about.

If I've learned anything on my journey it's that you should always be you. Be kind to others, and to yourself. Do what you can't, and don't let other people tell you who you are. Live your best life, whatever that means for you. You don't have to try and be what you see on Instagram. Most of that shit is fake, anyway. What makes you happy may not be what makes other people happy, so don't let them tell you what you should do with your life. Follow your heart, follow your passions and live the life that was meant for you.

No apologies.

ACKNOWLEDGEMENTS

I would like to acknowledge my family, especially my dad, big Markos, for raising me to be a strong, independent woman and to challenge the status quo.

Thank you to my whole family for championing me in the brightest times, and showing me the light during my darkest days. Kathryn Deiliou, my amazing manager since 2011, you are an absolute go-getter and leader in a male-dominated industry; we make the best team and I couldn't have done life outside of sport without you. Also the rest of the TLA team – in particular Boxy, Tom and Jack for always having my back.

Martin and the team at Affirm Press for taking a chance, believing in me and backing me. Fiona Harris, for being the empowering strong woman you are and for helping my dreams of creating this book to come true.

Last, but definitely not least, my new husband as of 1.1.21, Luke Norder. Marrying you topped the list of everything I have done in my life thus far, you are my best friend and I love you so much. Here's to our next chapter, baby.

To all of you who I haven't mentioned – you know who you are. My fans/Sharni Army. My support network. My inner sanctum. My forever people. I love you X.

ABOUT FIONA HARRIS

Fiona is the co-creator and writer of the internationally award-winning comedy web series *The Drop-off*. With her husband, Mike McLeish, she adapted the series into an adult fiction novel which was released in May 2020. The series will broadcast as a telemovie for Nine Network. She is the author of several children's books, including *The Super Moopers*, *Trolls* and *Miraculous* series.

Fiona co-wrote and starred in TV sketch comedy shows including *SkitHouse*, *Flipside* and *Comedy Inc – The Late Shift*, and her numerous acting credits include *The Beautiful Lie*, *Upright*, *Tangle*, *Mr & Mrs Murder*, *The Time of Our Lives*, *Offspring*, *Beaconsfield* and *The Librarians*.

Fiona's dad was team manager for the Melbourne Football Club for thirty years, so she has spent more than her fair share of time growing up in smelly club rooms! In addition to *No Apologies*, Fiona has three other books due for release in 2021: *The Pick-up* (sequel to *The Drop-off*), AFL star Marcus Bontempelli's picture book, and a series of junior fiction books. To learn more about Fiona, please visit fionaharris.com.